Functional Units

Activating Vocabulary

Mark Fletcher and Roger Hargreaves

Nelson

Thomas Nelson and Sons Ltd
Nelson House Mayfield Road
Walton-on-Thames Surrey
KT12 5PL UK

51 York Place
Edinburgh
EH1 3JD UK

Thomas Nelson (Hong Kong) Ltd
Toppan Building 10/F
22A Westlands Road
Quarry Bay Hong Kong

First published by Evans Brothers Limited 1980
(Under ISBN 0 237 50421 9)
Reprinted once

Second impression published by Unwin Hyman Limited 1984
(Under ISBN 0 7135 2404 9)

Third impression published by Thomas Nelson and Sons Limited 1989

ISBN 0-17-555816-7
NPN 9 8 7 6 5 4 3 2

Illustrated by Mark Fletcher

The authors would like to thank Peter O'Connell and the staff at the School of English Studies, Folkestone, for suggestions and improvements to *Activating Vocabulary* in its pilot form.

Printed in Hong Kong

Contents

Introduction 2
1. Family and Pets 5
2. My Home 7
3. The House and Garden 9
4. Household Tasks 13
5. In the Pub 15
6. In the Post Office 17
7. Shopping 19
8. Clothes 22
9. People 24
10. Health 26
11. Food 28
12. The Weather 31
13. Holidays 34
14. Travel by Plane, Train and Boat 36
15. Hitch-hiking and Camping 38
16. On the Road 40
17. Motoring 42
18. Hotels 44
19. Sightseeing in London 46
20. Country and Farm 49
21. Buildings: Town, Suburban, Industrial and Historic 51
22. Postcards and Letters 54
23. Hobbies 56
24. Parties 58
25. Theatre and Shows 60
26. In the Restaurant 62
27. Keeping Fit 64
28. Football and Tennis 66
29. Sports 68
30. Customs and Festivals 70
31. Newspapers 72
32. Television and Radio 74
33. Telephone 76
34. Education 78
35. Jobs 80
36. Interviews and Job Prospects 82
37. Meetings and Conferences 84
38. Sales, Production and Distribution 86
39. Bank and Money 88
40. Standard of Living 90
Glossary 92

Introduction

PURPOSE AND APPROACH

The book is intended to make vocabulary learning an active process, in which the student uses his or her knowledge and imagination to contribute to the work of the class. The material has been arranged in topics so that it can be used selectively according to the needs and level of the students. Interest is maintained by practising the new vocabulary through a variety of entertaining and useful activities.

THE TOPICS

The units cover situations in which the students will find themselves (e.g. Shopping, Parties, Meetings and Conferences) and also topics they will want to talk about (e.g. Hobbies, Food, Standard of Living).

The subjects fall into four broad categories: things to do with the *student* and the *local environment* (1–12), things to do with *travel* (13–22), things to do with *entertainment* (23–32) and things to do with *work* (33–40).

THE LEVEL

Parts of the very early units are quite elementary and act as a check on basic points which intermediate students should already be familiar with. A few of the later ones will stretch quite advanced students (e.g. Newspapers, TV and Radio, Bank and Money). The majority of units however, are aimed at enriching the vocabulary of intermediate students working up towards First Certificate level.

USING THE UNITS

A unit can be used as material for a vocabulary lesson, or as a good introduction to a discussion or to project work on a related topic. It can also serve as an interesting way of checking that students do have sufficient active command of essential vocabulary to be able to talk and write about the various key topics.

The format of the units is varied but they all aim to provide, and to make the student use, key vocabulary. Important words and phrases are given, followed by material designed to check that the student understands them, activities to practise using the vocabulary in context (usually orally) and writing exercises for consolidation.

Vocabulary and phrases This section is best treated initially as an informal activity with the teacher reading through the phrases, encouraging questions, asking for and giving explanations, relating, and encouraging students to help each other relate, new material to familiar vocabulary.

When the meaning has been established, students should read out items to practise pronunciation and to provide a second opportunity to check understanding. Where the material is presented in the form of questions with a variety of alternative replies, the students should be encouraged to work in pairs, building up conversations around the phrases supplied.

Word checks These are really tests that words are known, and usually involve putting the right words to numbered pictures. In some cases a list of words is supplied and the students make a choice (e.g. Units 3 to 8); in other units the vocabulary can be found by referring back to the text (e.g. Units 12 to 14); and in some (e.g. Units 20 and 21) students will have to draw on their collective knowledge to find some of the answers.

It is a good idea to let the students work through these word checks in small groups, pooling their knowledge. This makes a very student-centred activity and gives everyone a chance to contribute. Then an element of competition can be introduced by doing the checking as a team game with the groups asking and answering questions, e.g. *What is number 7 please? It's a rug.* (Unit 3), scoring points for right answers and bonus points for answering when mistakes are made by the other groups. The teacher acts as referee.

To talk about Under this heading there are questions and topics for further discussion. They can be worked at in small groups, or given as a written homework exercise.

Activity Under this general heading come a number of activities, including tasks, short talks to prepare, points for discussion, mini role-playing situations, descriptions of processes, fill-in-the-blank and odd-man-out exercises, quizzes, puzzles and questionnaires. All are designed to refer the student to the vocabulary of the unit and to encourage him or her to see it in context and actually *use* it. Most of the exercises are short, but the tasks, e.g. Olympic Games (Unit 29) and Think of a Product (Unit 38) do generate a lot of discussion, as do talks about subjects like Hobbies (Unit 23) and Customs and Festivals (Unit 30).

At the end of each Activity Section there are a few words or phrases to be incorporated into short dialogues. The students should be encouraged to make the meaning clear from the context of the dialogue. It is a good idea for students to write a dialogue in pairs and then read it out. (This exercise often highlights points for useful remedial work.)

Note Most of the vocabulary in this book will be found in a good English language dictionary and teachers and students are advised to keep one at hand for reference. Some of the more difficult and culturally linked words are explained in the **Glossary** on pages 92–93.

1 Family and Pets

Are you married or single? — I'm married.
Have you got any children? — Yes, I've got a daughter aged 6 and a son of 3. How about you?

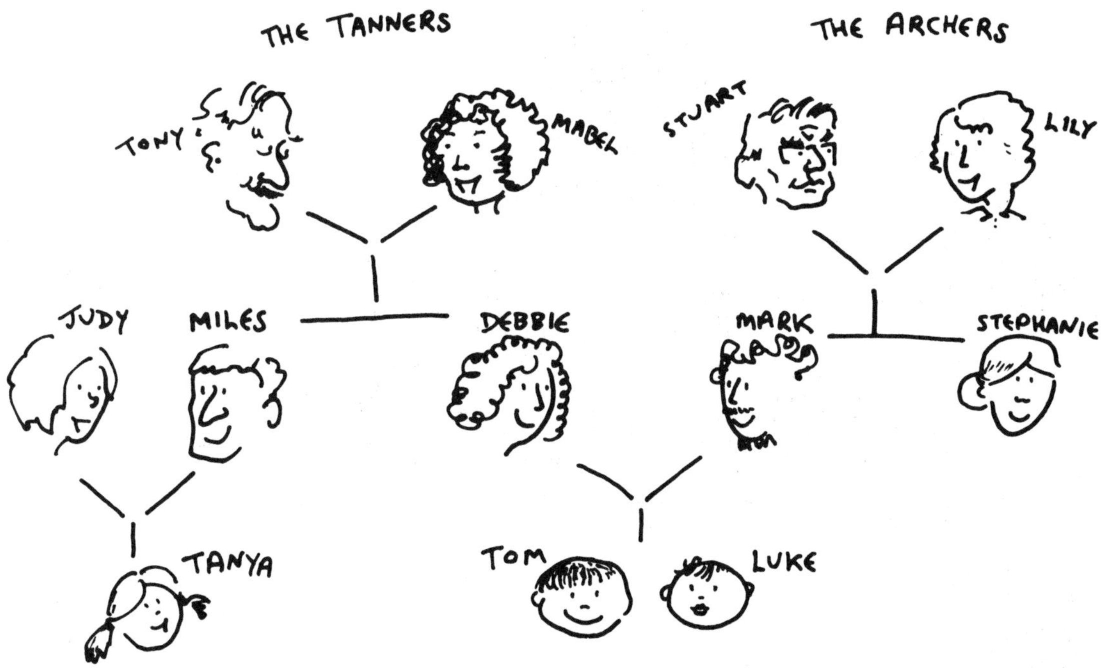

WORD CHECK

Who's who

How quickly can you find out (the words on page 6 will help):

Tony is Mark's ....
What relation is Tom to Stuart?
Who is Mark's niece?
Judy is Miles's ....
Miles is Mark's ....
Stephanie is Luke's ....
Tom and Tanya are ....
What relation is Luke to Judy?
Debbie is Lily's ....
Has Tom got an uncle?

Relatives

mother, father, son,
daughter, grandfather,
grandmother, uncle,
aunt, nephew, niece,
cousin, sister-in-law,
brother-in-law, mother-in-law,
father-in-law, grandson,
granddaughter,
husband, wife.

Other members of the family – pets!

cat
canary
Alsatian dog
goldfish
guinea pig*
rabbit
poodle*
pony
mouse
tortoise
kitten
puppy

Which two of these pets would you like? Why?
What are the disadvantages of the others?

ACTIVITY

1. **Draw your own family tree and describe it to your neighbour.**
2. **Write a short dialogue using the words:**
   uncle grandmother pet

2 My Home

Work with the student next to you on the following questions:

Where do you live?

I live in ...., an industrial town.

It's
- a small town
- a village
- an old city
- a modern city
- a port

- in ....
- near ....
- on the coast of ....
- on the River ....

What's the countryside like?

The area is
- flat.
- mountainous.
- hilly.
- very industrial.
- built up.

The countryside is
- very pretty.
- rather dull.

What sort of town is it?

The town has
- a university
- good shops.
- a good night life.
- an interesting old port.
- lots of places to visit.

It's very
- quiet.
- busy.

It's full of
- factories.
- traffic.
- tourists.
- students.
- retired people.

①

②

③

What kind of house do you live in?

I live in a
- terraced house (1).
- detached house (2).
- flat (3).

How far is your house from the . . .?	It's {two miles from / very near / not far from} {the town centre. / the harbour. / the shopping centre.}
What's it like?	It's {old/modern. / quiet/noisy. / comfortable/uncomfortable. / tidy/untidy.} It has a big garden. There isn't a garden.
What do people do?	Most people {work in offices/factories. / commute to the big cities.}
Is there much to do in the evenings?	There {'s a lot to do. / isn't a lot to do.}
	People {go for a stroll in the evenings. / stay at home.}
What do *you* do?	I enjoy fishing and going to the pub.

What's the difference between the following? Can you draw them?
detached, semi-detached, terraced house, bungalow, flat, bedsitter.

ACTIVITY

1. **Interview someone about themselves and their home for five minutes. Then they will interview you. Take notes. Then give a one-minute report on the other person to the class.**
2. **Write a short dialogue using the words:**
   detached house   industrial   near

3 The House and Garden

WORD CHECK

Put the number with the word:

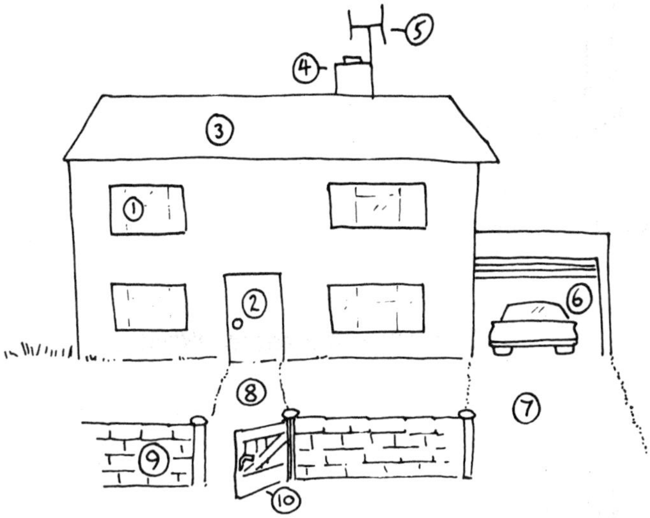

gate ___, drive ___, chimney ___, aerial ___, roof ___, garage ___, path ___, window ___, front door ___, wall ___.

downstairs ___, dining room ___, cellar ___, upstairs ___, kitchen ___, bedroom ___, attic ___, bathroom ___, living room ___, toilet ___.

wall ___, ceiling ___, floor ___, landing ___, stairs ___, hall ___.

Living room

cosy, nicely decorated

Describe this room. What's it like?

Kitchen

Is this kitchen well equipped?
Is it cramped?
Does it have lots of working surfaces?

Bedroom
comfortable, nice view
lots of cupboard space

Is this like your bedroom?

Garden
well laid out
flowers and vegetables

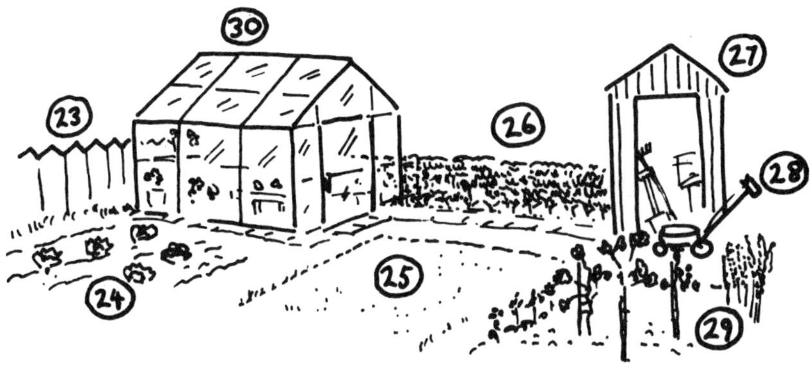

Have you got a garden?
What do you grow in it?
Is a garden essential?

Put the number to the name:
shed ___, sink ___, bedside table ___, chest of drawers ___, lawn ___, bookshelves ___, fridge ___, ornaments ___, carpet ___, fence ___, sheet ___, lamp ___, pillow ___, electric fire ___, draining board ___, hedge ___, rug ___, flowerbed ___, dressing gown ___, greenhouse ___, wardrobe ___, oven ___, vegetable garden ___, lawnmower ___, blanket ___, armchair ___, teatowel ___, sofa ___, coffee table ___, cupboard ___.

Keeping warm

How do you keep warm at home in winter?

Have you got central heating?
gas/electric/coal (open) fires?
double glazing*?

ACTIVITY

Write a short dialogue using the words:
decorated comfortable bookshelves

4 Household Tasks

Housework

What are these people doing?

Look at Picture 5.

Can I help with the washing up? Thanks very much. The teatowel's* over there.

Ask someone if you can help with the other jobs. These words will help:
peeler, bucket, dishcloth, polish, clean sheets, table mats, saucepan, broom, teatowel, Hoover*, clothes basket, pegs.

D.I.Y. (Do it Yourself) The handyman with his tool kit

I can { put up shelves, lay linoleum* (lino),
plaster cracks, hang wallpaper,
change a washer,
drill holes, replace light bulbs,
mix concrete, paint walls,
stick the broken bits together again.

Which of these things can you do?
What do you need for these jobs?

Can you find these in your classroom:
a plug, a hinge, some pipe, a switch, some flex, a screw, a joint?

What needs mending?
The windows need replacing.
The cracks ...

What do you use these for?

ACTIVITY

1. **Work in small groups.**

   You have £500 to spend on electrical appliances. What would you buy to save as much time as possible on the housework?

Automatic washing machine	£250	Electric drill and accessories	£50
Deep-freeze	£300	Hoover	£100
Electric mixer	£50	Refrigerator	£130
Dishwasher	£100	Portable TV	£100

2. **Write a short dialogue using the words:**
   broken replace stick

5 In the Pub

Pub signs

Buying drinks for people

This is on me. (Makes it clear *you're* going to pay.)
This is my round. (You're paying for a group.)

What'll you have?/What would you like? I'll have a {pint of bitter / gin and tonic. / half of Guinness*. / Coca Cola.}

(to the barman) A half of Guinness and . . ., please.

Facts about pubs

Ordinary beer's called *bitter*. Look for the CAMRA (Campaign for Real Ale) signs for the best traditional bitter.

Licensing (opening) hours* are: 10.30–14.30
18.00–22.30 on weekdays, and
12.00–14.00
19.00–22.30 on Sundays.

Price list

Bitter	. . . . pint	80p
	. . . . $\frac{1}{2}$ pint	40p
Scotch	. . . .	70p
Guinness	. . . . pint	90p
Lager	. . . . pint	80p
Gin	. . . .	70p
Soft drinks	. . . .	40p
Tonic/soda, ginger ale	. . . .	40p

Snacks

WORD CHECK

Put the number with the word:
sandwich ___,
peanuts ___,
a packet of crisps ___,
pickled eggs ___.

Pub games

TO TALK ABOUT

What is the equivalent of a pub in your country?
What do you drink there?
Can you sing/dance/get food/ stay very late?
Can children go in? Do women go alone?

ACTIVITY

1. **Four of you have arrived in a pub. Go to the bar and order drinks.**
2. **Write a short dialogue using the words:**
   crisps bitter closing time

6 In the Post Office

Can I have { stamps for these postcards to Japan please?
Can I have { a stamp for a letter to Mexico please?
Can I have { three 10p stamps please?

How much is it to send this to Brazil please?

Can I send this telegram please?

You want to send a) a parcel
b) a postcard
c) a telegram to the USA. **What do you say to the post office clerk?**

WORD CHECK

Find the word for each number:

1. . . . . 5. . . . .
2. . . . . 6. . . . .
3. . . . . 7. . . . .
4. . . . . 8. . . . .

notepaper, air letter, registered mail, postman, post office clerk, counter, scales, letter-box (post box).

address a letter, get (receive) a letter, stick a stamp on, seal the envelope;
tie up a parcel (Sellotape*, string), weigh it, post it;
fill in a form, buy a postal order, collect old age pension/child allowance*, get a TV/dog licence.

What do these people do to get a letter to its destination?
a) the sender
b) the post office clerk
c) the postman

ACTIVITY

1. Telegrams

In pairs work out what these telegrams mean:

a) SORRY MISSED PLANE MEET BA776 HEATHROW 14TH SUGGEST POSTPONE MEETING PHONING TONIGHT JENKINS

b) YOURS 14/4 YOU QUOTE TWENTY PERCENT OFF LIST PRICE MAXIMUM TEN PERCENT ACCEPTABLE ADVISE ROTTERDAM REP DIRECT WRITING THOMSON

c) HOTEL BURGLED SEND £150 SOONEST CREDIT LYONNAIS NANTES INFORM COLLEGE RETURN IMPOSSIBLE BEFORE MONDAY ANNE

2. **Write a short dialogue using the words:**
post box parcel deliver

7 Shopping

Ask the person next to you about their watch, bag, pen, coat, and something else they have.

Where did you get that hat?

How much { did it cost? / was it?

Can I help you? — Just looking thanks.
Yes, have you got a . . .?
Can I try this on please?
Can I have a look at that one?

Where to shop

Supermarket (large shop – basically for food but often sells other things as well), e.g. *Sainsbury's*, *Tesco's*: long rows of shelves, trolleys, wire baskets, special offers, wide range of goods, check-out counters, trading stamps, impulse buying, 2p off.

Chain store (shops with a branch in most towns), e.g. *Marks and Spencer's, Woolworth's, Boots.*

Department store (very big shop with a wide range of goods – usually clothing, furnishing etc.), e.g. *Selfridges, Harrods.*

Corner shop (little shop often owned and run by a family): friendly atmosphere, personal service, helpful assistants, more expensive.

Where are these people shopping?

1

2

3

What are the advantages of shopping in a department store?
Do you prefer shopping in a corner shop or a supermarket?

Going shopping

shopping centre, window shopping, sale, bargain, very good value, reduced, shopping list, book token, gift voucher, receipt, look at, sold out, cash desk, early closing day, pay cash, pay by cheque, pay by credit card, hire purchase.

How do you carry your shopping home?
shopping bag, basket, carrier bag, paper bag, cardboard box, 'Wrap it up please.'

ACTIVITY

1. Picnic shopping list

Work in groups of three.
You are buying things for a picnic.

a) Ask 'How much is/are . . .' questions.
b) You have £2.50 to buy a picnic for three people – make your choice. (Remember that although some prices are quoted per kilo you can buy less than a kilo.)

Coca Cola	30p per can
Bread	35p per loaf (small)
Ham	41p per 100 g
Cheese	£2.80 per kilo
Tomatoes	60p per kilo
Lettuce	20p each
Chocolate	20p per 100 g
Orange juice	38p per large bottle
Eggs (for hard boiling)	55p per dozen
Light ale	35p per can
Wine	£3.55 per bottle
Apples	95p per kilo
Oranges	8p each
Bananas	84p per kilo
Biscuits	18p per packet
Sausage rolls*	16p each
Crisps	7p per packet
Pork pies	22p each

2. **Where can you get**
1. a doughnut and a sausage roll?
2. some Stilton, some Cheddar and some Leicester*?
3. shoe polish?
4. shampoo?
5. pâté?
6. a light bulb?
7. some orange squash*?

At the moment these shops are selling the wrong things.
Put the right goods in the right shops:

Shop		
Grocer's	A.	soap, medicines, pills, bandages, cosmetics.
Butcher's	B.	tools, detergents, oil, paraffin, heaters, cutlery.
Fishmonger's	C.	meat, poultry, game, sausages.
Greengrocer's	D.	bread, cakes, pies, biscuits.
Baker's	E.	radios, TVs, electric kettles, heaters, lights, bulbs, batteries, wire and cable, switches.
Dairy	F.	cigarettes, tobacco, pipes, lighters, cigars, matches.
Tobacconist's	G.	milk, eggs, butter.
Chemist's	H.	mackerel, cod, trout, lobster.
Delicatessen	I.	cleaning things, food in tins and packets, soft drinks (soft = non-alcoholic).
Hardware store	K.	fruit, nuts, fresh vegetables.
Electrician's	L.	foreign foods, herbs, spices, tea and coffee.

3. **Write a short dialogue using the words:**
window shopping   carrier bag   delicatessen

8 Clothes

What do you usually wear for work?
a party?
a football match?
a picnic?

get { dressed/undressed | changed | ready to go out }

put on/take off { a coat | boots | swimming trunks }

WORD CHECK

Put the number with the word:
skirt ___, cardigan ___, vest ___, shirt ___, pullover ___, slippers ___, handkerchief ___, roll-neck pullover ___, briefs ___, belt ___, shorts ___, bra ___, cufflinks ___, socks ___, dress ___, trousers ___, tie ___, tights ___, pants ___, blouse ___, jeans ___.

It's January. It's snowing. Fred has to walk to work. What should he put on?
It's a lovely sunny August day. What should Liz put on to go shopping?

Compliments

I like your new tie.
That's a very smart jacket.
That suits you.
What a pretty dress.

Describing clothes

striped, checked, patterned, plain, spotted, floral print, wool, silk, cotton, nylon, corduroy, terylene.

What are you wearing?

Buying clothes

What size do you take?
Can I try this on?
Can I change this please?
It's a bit tight here.
They're too long/tight/small/big for me.
Have you got this in green?
I'll have this one.
I'll leave it, thanks.

Buy a T-shirt/a hat/a suit/a pair of shoes from your neighbour.

ACTIVITY

Write a short dialogue using the words:

tight   striped shirt   tie

9 People

Choose somebody in the class or somebody that you all know, e.g. a TV personality, film star etc. What's he/she like?
Describe someone you know/met yesterday.

What does he/she do? He's/She's a doctor/teacher/student.
What does he/she look like?

He	*He/She*	*She*
	looks about 26	has a nice figure
	is tall/average height	
is broad-shouldered	is well built/of medium build	
	is fat/thin/slim	is blonde/brunette
	is fair/dark (–haired)	has a good complexion
	is weatherbeaten/suntanned/pale	
	has a wide/small mouth	
	has a long/hooked/broad/snub nose	
	has blue/grey/green/brown eyes	
	has freckles/wrinkles	
has a beard/moustache	has long/short/curly/straight hair	
is bald	wears smart/trendy/casual/scruffy clothes	wears a lot of make-up
is handsome	is good looking	is beautiful/pretty

What are these people like?
very nice (pleasant), kind, friendly, good-natured,
clever (skilful), intelligent, bright,
'a bit thick'*, entertaining,
dull, generous, mean, nervous,
reserved, confident, aggressive,
extrovert (outgoing),
introvert (quiet),
ambitious, unambitious (easy-going),
calm, excitable, hot tempered,
severe-looking,
amusing, witty, a good talker,
gloomy, miserable,
optimistic, pessimistic.

ACTIVITY

1. Find your partner for life.

calm	6	very careful and thorough	3	ambitious	2
a lot of initiative	6	dreamy	2	very practical	3
very good looking	4	mean	1	formal in dress	6
rather shy	3	excitable	2	clever	5
generous	4	helpful	5	fashion conscious	2
casual in dress	2	independent	1	a good mixer	6
good humoured	1				
sporty	5				

Make a note of three of these qualities which apply to you. Add up their score.
Make a note of three qualities which you look for in a partner. Add up their score.
Add the two sums together.
Subtract 4 if you don't smoke. Subtract 2 if you don't drink alcohol.
Add 1 if you are tall.
Make a note of your final score.

Now, choose a colour: blue, grey, green, brown.

Everyone says their final score.

Anyone who has your score ±1: You have a lot in common. Sit next to each other for a few days and see what happens . . .

Anyone who has your score exactly: Do you feel your heart beating faster? This may be IT, the start of something BIG. Take a chance – the rest of us are watching with interest!

Anyone who has your score *and* the same colour: You have found your heart's desire. Romance is definitely here and (if you both like ice-cream and bananas for breakfast) it must be wedding bells!

2. **Write a short dialogue using the words:**
freckles excitable scruffy

10 Health

Practise in pairs:

You don't look very well. What's the matter?

I've got a { high temperature. / cold. / sore throat. / headache. / pain in my ... }

I've { cut my finger. / broken my leg. / hurt my shoulder. / twisted my knee. / bruised my arm. }

I feel { sick. / awful. / feverish. }

I'm sorry to hear that.

You'd better { see a doctor. / have a stiff drink. / go to bed. / take an aspirin/sleeping pill/pain killer. / put a bandage on it. }

How's your cold/headache?

It's { still there I'm afraid. / getting better thanks. / much better now thanks. }

I keep feeling dizzy. What can I do?

make an appointment ... go to the doctor's ... doctor's surgery* ... receptionist ... surgery is 8.30 a.m.–10.30 a.m. ... have a check-up.

What will the doctor do?

He'll { examine you. / take your temperature with a thermometer. / listen to your breathing with a stethoscope. / check your blood pressure/pulse rate/reflexes. / say, 'Open wide, put out your tongue and say "Aaah".' }

What will he give me?

a prescription/medicine (the dose: 1 teaspoonful three times a day)/pills/ointment/an injection.

What's wrong with you?

The doctor told you to: gargle with this three times a day.
come back in three weeks to have the plaster off.
stay out of contact with people for ten days.
keep an Elastoplast* on it and keep it dry for 48 hours.
eat no fried or fatty food, drink no alcohol and take no energetic exercise for six months.
get back to work at once.

In hospital

emergency, ambulance, stretcher, hospital, casualty department, men's/ women's/ children's ward, operating theatre, have an operation/anaesthetic, nurse, surgeon, consultant.

Visiting hours: 'How are you feeling today?' 'Get well soon.'

WORD CHECK

What's number 3? **What's wrong with Mr 16?**

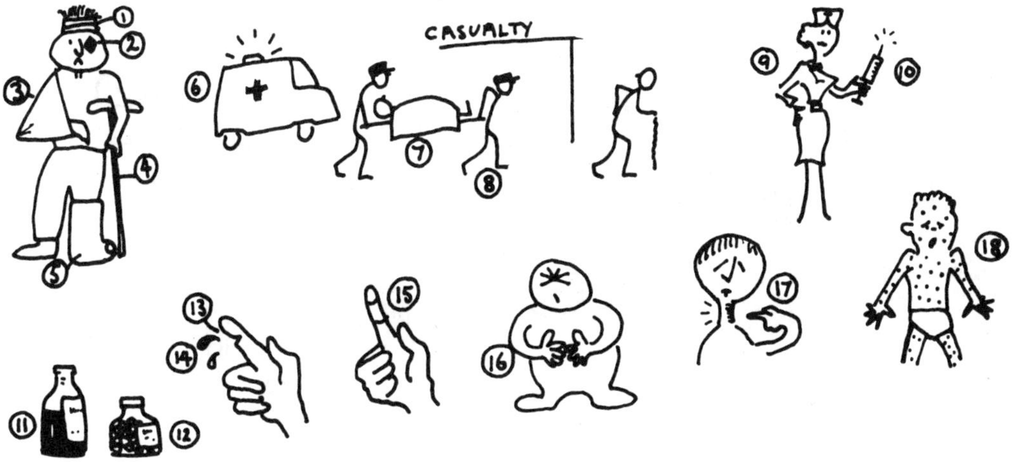

TO TALK ABOUT

Do you have a free medical service in your country? Is there a private system? Is good medical treatment easy to get? Is it expensive?

ACTIVITY

1. **In pairs:**
   a) phone the doctor's surgery and make an appointment.
   b) tell the doctor you feel terrible.
2. **Write a short dialogue using the words:**
   ache temperature prescription

11 Food

Remember:
You usually *have* a cup of tea (not: drink a cup of tea)
You usually *have* a sandwich (not: eat a sandwich)

Do you like curries?
salads?
stews*?

Some things you might have in England – not all on the same day!

Can you find meat pie, potatoes and peas?
steak and kidney pudding?
grapefruit?
apple pie and custard*?
marmalade*?
biscuits?
a boiled egg?
salad?

How things are cooked

boiled, fried, baked, steamed, grilled, sautéed; (and of course there are lots of things you eat raw)

Dinner with friends

Help yourself.
Do start.
Mmm – this pie is lovely.
Would you like some sauce/mustard?
Could you pass the salt please . . .?
You must let me have the recipe.
I love homemade bread.
Would you like some more . . .?
No thanks, that was absolutely delicious.
Can I take your plate?
Let me give you a hand with the washing up.

ACTIVITY

1. **You have invited some friends to dinner.**
   a) Choose the meal from the pictures on page 28.
   b) Serve your friends and make sure they get enough to eat.

2. **Is it true that in France people like frogs' legs?**
   in Saudi Arabia people like sheep's eyes?
   in Japan people like raw fish?
   Describe your national dish.

3. **Mixed pairs**
   Food often comes in pairs, like 'fish and chips'.

   Can you find the right partners?

apple pie	butter
roast beef	marmalade
bacon	champagne
toast	kidney
steak	eggs
oysters	biscuits
cheese	custard
bread	Yorkshire pudding*

4. A Recipe
   Explain how to make this simple dish from the pictures on page 30.

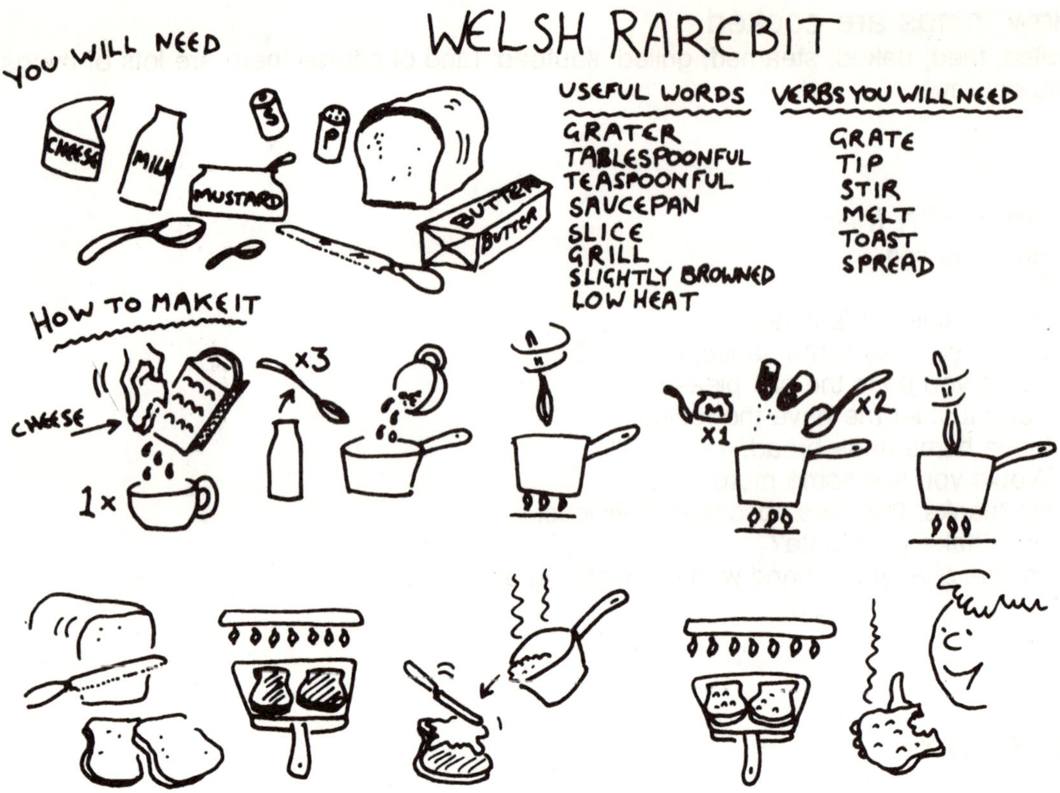

5. **Write a short dialogue using the words:**
fried pass rice delicious

12 The Weather

In England the weather is very changeable. You must always be ready to say something about the weather. Like this:

Nice/Lovely Warmer Colder Chilly Horrible	today, isn't it?

The usual reply is:
Yes, it is, isn't it?

Hot:

It's
- a lovely day.
- a bit sticky (humid, hot and wet).
- really hot.

Phew! What a scorcher!

Wet:

It's
- drizzling a bit.
- just a shower.
- raining quite hard.
- pouring down.

Cold:

It's
- a bit chilly.
- very cold.
- icy/freezing/bitter.

It's
- snowing.
- sleeting.
- frosty.

Other:

It's
- windy
- cloudy
- foggy
- stormy (thunder and lightning)

Extreme conditions

hurricane, typhoon, flood, heatwave, drought, avalanche.

WORD CHECK

What's the weather like here?

1

2

3

and here?

What's the weather like today?

Months

January
February
March
April
May
June
July
August
September
October
November
December

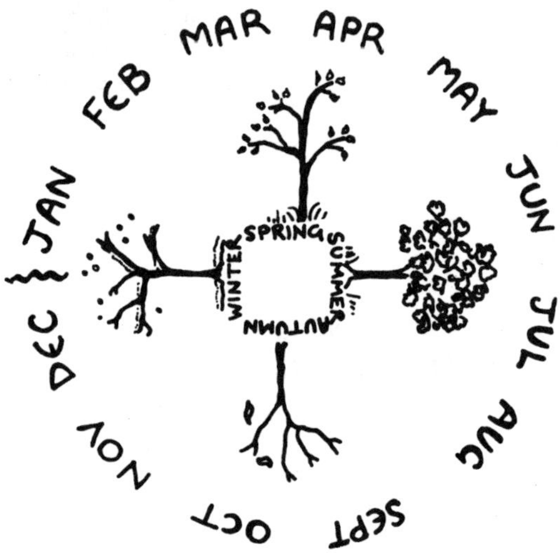

Seasons

Spring
Summer
Autumn
Winter

ACTIVITY

1. **Which countries have these weather conditions?**
   It's hot all the year round.
   There's a rainy season.
   It's very humid.
   It's dark most of the day in winter.
   There's a typhoon season.
   It's often foggy.
   There are heavy snowfalls.
   The summers are very hot and the winters are very cold.

2. Weather chart

		°C			°C
Algeria	s	21	Malta	s	18
Amsterdam	c	0	Montreal	s	−11
Athens	c	10	Moscow	sn	−9
Belgrade	s	−5	Munich	s	−4
Buenos Aires	s	25	New York	s	1
Brussels	c	1	Nice	c	12
Cologne	f	0	Oslo	c	−7
Copenhagen	f	2	Paris	fg	3
Edinburgh	c	0	Reykjavik	c	2
Geneva	c	3	Rome	s	15
Helsinki	s	−6	Stockholm	s	−4
Innsbruck	f	2	Tel Aviv	s	18
Las Palmas	s	20	Toronto	s	−9
London	s	3	Vienna	s	−6
Madrid	f	14	Zurich	c	−1
Malaga	s	19			

Key: c = cloudy; f = fair; r = rain; s = sunny; sn = snow; fg = fog.

What time of year do you think this is?

3. **Write a short dialogue using the words:**
a bit chilly autumn flood

13 Holidays

Ask the person next to you:

Did you go on holiday last year?
Where did you go?

I had
- a nice quiet relaxing holiday . . .
- a skiing/winter sports holiday . . .
- a camping/walking holiday . . .
- a sightseeing/touring holiday . . .
- a caravanning holiday . . .

. . . by the sea.
. . . in the mountains.
. . . in the countryside.
. . . in northern Italy.

What did you do?/How did you spend your holiday?

We
- stayed at home.
- went to visit relatives.
- took the children to the sea.
- went by plane/car to . . .
- rented a cottage.
- hired a boat on the canals.
- went on a package tour*.

What did you take?

I took
- warm clothes.
- swimming trunks/a bathing costume/a bikini.
- suntan oil.
- sunglasses.
- lots of luggage.

What was it like?

It rained all the time.
The weather was lovely.
We had a really nice time.
It was very interesting/enjoyable.
I'll never go there again!

Have you ever had a holiday like this?

It was cheap/expensive to stay there . . . lots to do in the evenings . . . a friendly atmosphere . . . the people were very friendly . . . I took a lot of photos . . . went sightseeing . . . looked around the museums . . . stayed for two weeks in a hotel . . . went swimming every day . . . drank a lot . . . tasted the local food . . . didn't like the food . . . couldn't speak the language . . . got a suntan . . . got sunburnt! . . . met a beautiful Swedish girl/fell in love with the waiter.

WORD CHECK

What sort of holiday are these people having?

ACTIVITY

Write a short dialogue using the words:
suntan   package holiday   sightseeing

14 Travel by Plane, Train and Boat

Did you have a good journey from Paris? Yes thanks. It was very easy.
How did you travel? I came by train and boat.

Go by { train (passenger).
plane (passenger).
car (driver/passenger).
bike (cyclist).

Go on foot (pedestrian).
Hitch-hike (hitch-hiker).

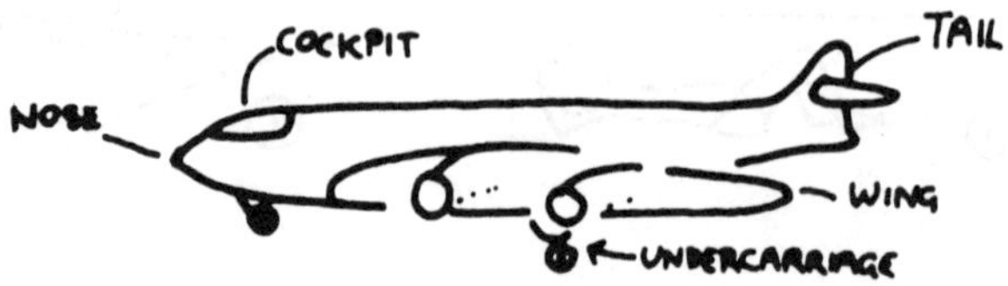

By plane

make a reservation, book a seat, buy a ticket, air terminal, check in, ground hostess, excess baggage charges, conveyor belt, first class (F), economy class (Y), runway, departure/arrival time, gangway, window seat, steward/stewardess, air hostess, flight crew, 'Fasten your safety belts please and no smoking', emergency exit, life jacket, take-off, altitude.
passenger service, pre-cooked food, duty free items, a bumpy flight, airsick.
'Arrival/departure has been delayed owing to a technical fault',
air traffic control (ATC), circling for hours, waiting to land, 'We're down',
passenger terminal, arrival/departure lounge, VIP lounge, immigration/passport control, Customs, 'My luggage has been lost/damaged/sent to the wrong place'.

ACTIVITY

Use some of this vocabulary and the pictures to tell the story of your flight.

By train

station, platform, ticket office, single/return ticket, book a seat, waiting room, loud-speaker, announcement, timetable, sleeper, first/second class compartment, dining car, buffet, luggage rack.

ACTIVITY

Using the pictures, describe a journey by train.

By boat

port/docks, go on board, ferry, car deck, passenger decks, cabins, the hold, cast off, rough/smooth crossing, foghorn, lifeboats, out of sight of land, the ship is rolling, 'I haven't got my sea legs yet!*' 'Have you got any sea sickness pills?'

Have you been on a hovercraft or a hydrofoil?

ACTIVITY

1. **Write about a journey you have made in a boat.**
2. **Write a short dialogue using the words:**
   luggage rough crossing reservation

15 Hitch-hiking and Camping

Hitch-hiking

It's adventurous and cheap!
You walk out of town and start thumbing ...

If you're lucky,
- you get picked up quickly.
- you get a good lift.
- drivers are very friendly.
- you meet interesting people.
- drivers buy you meals.
- you get put down in a good place for hitching.

What happens if you're unlucky?

You're standing by the road. Cars are rushing past. You don't know who will stop or where you'll be tonight. Perhaps you'll be in a youth hostel* or cheap hotel, or perhaps you'll still be waiting by the roadside.
Have you ever been in this situation? When?
What do you need? a rucksack
perhaps a groundsheet and sleeping bag
anything else?

TO TALK ABOUT

Have you ever hitch-hiked? Do you think it's safe? How long do you think it takes to hitch from Paris to Istanbul? Which way would you go? Which three cities would you most like to see? What problems would you expect? Which countries are difficult for hitch-hikers?

Camping

You can find your own camp site in a wood or field.
A good one is sheltered, quiet, flat, with a good view, good water and wood supplies.
Or you can go to a big organized camp site with water laid on and washing and cooking facilities.

Pitching the tent

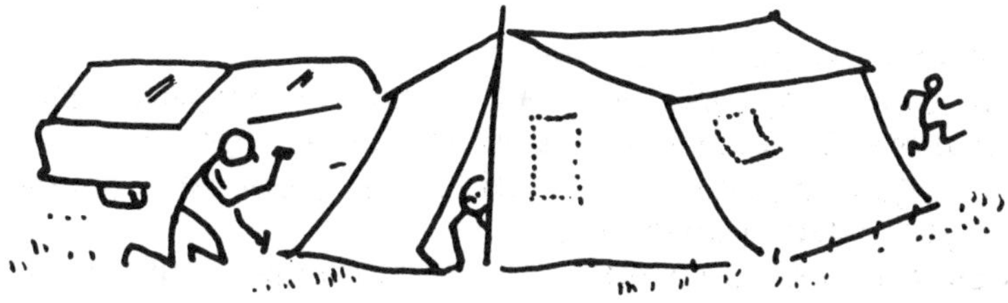

Put up the frame/tent poles and tighten the guy ropes. Hammer in the pegs.

ACTIVITY

1. **Make a list of 5 good things about camping. Make a list of 5 bad things about camping.**

2. **Write a short dialogue using the words:**
   thumb a lift   a long wait   soaking wet

16 On the Road

Motorists

cars, vans, lorries/trucks, container lorries, buses, coaches,
main road, dual carriageway, motorway, by-pass, ring road, lay-by, inside/outside lane.
zebra crossing, roundabout, crossroads, junction, diversion, roadworks, flyover, underpass, traffic jam, exhaust fumes, garage/petrol station, road signs, speed limit, double yellow lines*, traffic warden*, get a ticket, parking fine.
no entry, one-way street, access only, parking limited to . . . , parking meter, multi-storey car park.

Pedestrians

pavement, kerb, 'Look right, look left, look right again, cross the road', an island, pedestrian shopping area/precinct, school crossing patrol/lollipop lady*.

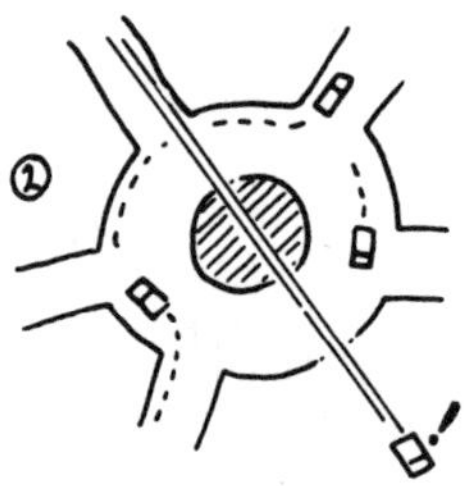

WORD CHECK

What are: 1. . . . .
2. . . . .
3. . . . .
4. . . . .
5. . . . .
6. . . . .

What do these signs mean?

TO TALK ABOUT

What are the main problems of driving in England?
There are many other countries where 'Drive on the left' is the rule. Can you name 5?
How tough are the traffic police/traffic wardens in your country?

ACTIVITY

Write a short dialogue using the words:
parking meter   parking fine   main road

17 Motoring

What sort of car have you got?

It's a red Morris 1300 . . .1974 model . . . economical to run . . . very reliable but the body-work's getting rusty in places.

It's a blue Ford Cortina . . . 'P' registration* . . . nice and roomy . . . good road holding . . . but a bit heavy on petrol.

get in, start up, drive off, change gear, go into third/fourth gear, accelerate, overtake/pass, park, reverse, brake, put the handbrake on, skid, crash, break down, call the AA*, scrape the paintwork, dent the wing, break the speed limit, traffic police, traffic wardens, parking offence, get a fine, flat tyre, run out of petrol, thumb a lift, learner, 'L' plates*, pass the driving test, MOT* test.

Did you have a good journey?

driving conditions, slippery surface, poor visibility, heavy traffic, stuck in a traffic jam.

Have you ever had trouble in a car? What happened?
How difficult is the driving test in your country?

WORD CHECK

Look at the pictures and find the words for the numbers.
horn ___, number plate ___, fuel gauge ___, accelerator ___, roof rack ___, windscreen ___, switches ___, clutch ___, boot ___, speedometer ___, indicator ___, hubcap ___, handbrake ___, headlights ___, wing mirror ___, steering wheel ___, milometer ___, driving mirror ___, gear lever ___, tyre ___, brake ___, windscreen wipers ___, bumper ___, radiator grill ___.

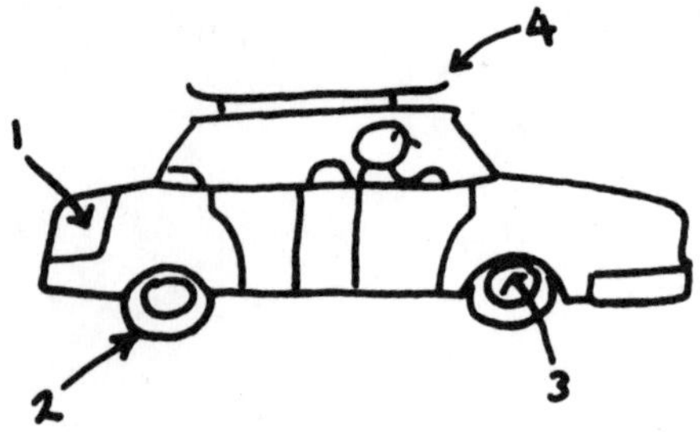

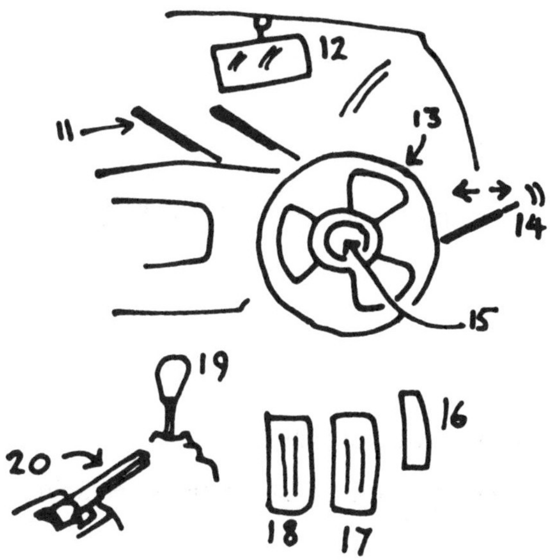

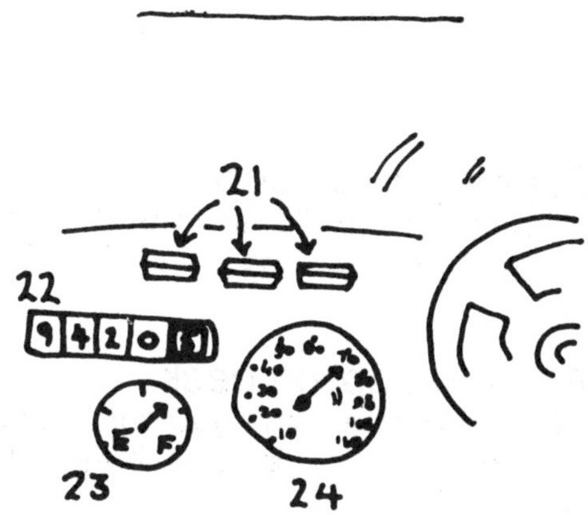

ACTIVITY

1. **In small groups, put the selling points for the Ford Striker in order of importance:**
   A. Good suspension
   B. Economic on petrol
   C. Rear windscreen wipers
   D. Large boot
   E. Reinforced steel chassis
   F. Car radio
   G. Good manoeuvrability
   H. Fully reclining seats
   I. Good servicing and spare parts network
   J. Automatically controlled sunroof and windows

2. **Write about either:**
   a) your car.
   b) a difficult journey in a car.

3. **Write a short dialogue using the words:**
   skid   change gear   speed limit

18 Hotels

Booking in advance

Good evening. I'd like to book a double room with bath for Friday 13th. The name's Crippen. C . . R . . I . . P . . P . . E . . N

At the reception desk

Good evening. Have you got a single room for two or perhaps three nights please?

With or without bath?

Without please.

We've got one at £15 a night, including breakfast.

That's fine.

Types of hotel

5 star hotel (*****), 4, 3, 2, 1 star; guest house; bed and breakfast (B & B).

In what kind of hotel would you find a: 24-hour room service*?
night club?
friendly atmosphere?
very big breakfast?
car hire service?
queue to get to the bathroom?

Types of room

double; single; twin bed; with or without bath; bed and breakfast; full board: evening meal.

People you might meet

receptionist, doorman, porter, waiter, chambermaid/cleaning lady.

On arrival
ask about room, check in, sign the guest book, get your key, go up in the lift, unpack.

On leaving
pack, ask for the bill, pay, check out.

In pairs, practise enquiring about a room, checking into a hotel and checking out.

ACTIVITY

1. Hotel survey

What was the last hotel you stayed in or visited like?
Was the room warm and comfortable? Did it have a lift/a bar/a nice view?
Give the hotel a mark out of 5 for good value:

Price:	Very reasonable	**5 4 3 2 1 0**	Much too expensive
Food:	Good and plenty of it	**5 4 3 2 1 0**	Awful
Service:	Friendly and efficient	**5 4 3 2 1 0**	Slow and rude
Facilities:	Good	**5 4 3 2 1 0**	Poor

17–20	Excellent value
12–17	Quite a good place to stay
8–12	Not really recommended
Less than **8**	Horrible

2. **Write a short dialogue using the words:**
full board receptionist very reasonable

19 Sightseeing in London

What should I do first?

Go up to town . . . Charing Cross . . . Trafalgar Square and Nelson's Column . . . lots of pigeons and sightseers taking photos . . . National Gallery . . . one of the world's finest collections of paintings . . . museums and art galleries are free. Visit the British Museum with its priceless treasures.

Tell me what to see in the centre?

Horse Guards Parade . . . Buckingham Palace with the Changing of the Guard . . . if the flag is flying the Queen is at home. Houses of Parliament, and Westminster Abbey where the kings, queens, famous writers, explorers, soldiers and statesmen are buried.

Where can I get a real impression of London?

Hyde Park and Speakers' Corner, colourful characters on soapboxes . . . a symbol of free speech . . . Regent's Park open air theatre . . . going round the Zoo.
Lunchtime in St James's Park . . . office workers with sandwiches feeding the ducks and thousands sunbathing in summer. Down river by boat, the Tower of London with its bloody history of murder and execution . . . the Crown Jewels are there now. The City of London . . . financial centre . . . the Bank of England and the Stock Exchange . . . the whole area empty after 5 o'clock when the commuters go home.

St Paul's with its great dome, and Wren's churches built after the Great Fire destroyed much of London in 1666 . . . the Monument, fish market and old spice wharves make it a place full of interest.

Where should I go shopping?

Bustling shopping crowds in Oxford Street and Regent Street . . . always busy but especially before Christmas or during the January sales. Petticoat Lane* where you might strike a bargain.

How can I travel around?

Up and down escalators to get the tube . . . so busy at rush hours . . . red buses . . . black taxis . . . sore feet . . . sightseeing is exhausting!

What is special about London?

It's such a cosmopolitan city . . . Chinese, Italians, West Indian areas . . . visitors and students from all over the world.

What is there to do at night?

Piccadilly Circus . . . Soho for nightlife, strip clubs, cabaret and dancing. A huge variety of restaurants. Go to a show in the West end . . . about forty theatres in the square mile between Shaftesbury Avenue and Aldwych. Theatre-goers in evening dress for First Nights. Queues at the big cinemas in Leicester Square. Go for a walk along the Embankment by the Thames . . . lights showing in the river.

ACTIVITY

1. **What happens** at Speakers' Corner?
   in Petticoat Lane?
   in the City?
   in Horseguards Parade?
   in Soho?
2. **Where might you go** Christmas shopping?
   to see a collection of Greek sculptures?
   for an interesting choice of restaurants?
   to see a play?
3. **Make a list of five advantages and five disadvantages of living in big cities.**
4. **Ask a friend to give you advice about sightseeing in a famous city.**
5. **Write a short dialogue using the words:**
   museum   cosmopolitan   rush hour

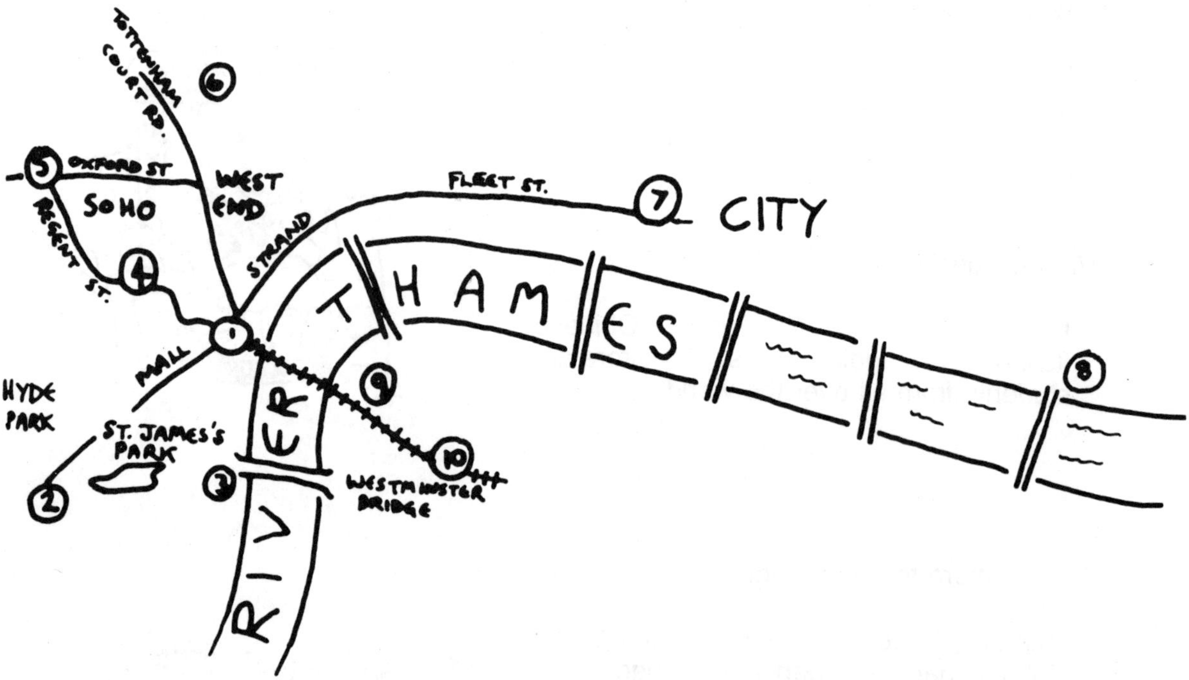

1. Charing Cross – Trafalgar Square
2. Buckingham Palace
3. Houses of Parliament – Westminster Abbey
4. Piccadilly Circus
5. Oxford Circus
6. British Museum
7. St Paul's Cathedral
8. Tower of London
9. Royal Festival Hall
10. Waterloo

20 Country and Farm

Is there any countryside near your home? What's it like?

Areas: hilly, mountainous, low lying, marshy, wooded, coastal areas.
Rivers: source, waterfall, bends, tributaries, estuary.
Woods/forests: conifers (evergreens, e.g. pine, fir), deciduous (e.g. oak, chestnut), plantations.
Rural area: fields, lanes, hedgerows, wildlife, conservation.

On the farm

arable land, ploughing, sowing, fertilizer, spraying, pest control, harvesting.

Some crops: wheat, barley, oats (corn);
turnips, parsnips, sugarbeet* (root vegetables);
lettuce, tomatoes (market gardening);
and fruit in the orchard.

Some livestock: dairy herd, beef cattle, bull, cow, calf (cattle);
chickens, ducks, turkeys (poultry).
sheep, goats, pigs.

Some machinery and equipment: tractor, plough, combine harvester, generator, milking machine, incubator, electric fences.

The farmyard

Outbuildings: barn, cowshed, henhouse, stables, silo, hayrick.

WORD CHECK

Find the word for each number:

1. ....
2. ....
3. ....
4. ....
5. ....
6. ....
7. ....
8. ....

TO TALK ABOUT

What types of farming are important in your country?
Is most of the farming on a large or small scale?
Are the types of farming and the methods changing?
The countryside looks nice on a sunny day, but would you really like to live there?

ACTIVITY

Write a short dialogue using the words:
plough harvest orchard

21 Buildings: Town, Suburban, Industrial and Historic

WORD CHECK

How quickly can you name the places?

1. . . . .
2. . . . .
3. . . . .
4. . . . .
5. . . . .
6. . . . .
7. . . . .
8. . . . .
9. . . . .
10. . . . .
11. . . . .
12. . . . .

Which of these can be found in your town?

town centre, suburbs, parks, playgrounds, playing fields.

redevelopment*, building sites, foundations, scaffolding, bulldozers, cranes, cement mixers.

avenues, roads, streets, alleys, paths.

fashionable/unfashionable areas, office blocks, blocks of flats, terraced houses, detached houses, semi-detached houses, council estates (houses owned by the local council), slums, warehouses, factories.

Historic buildings

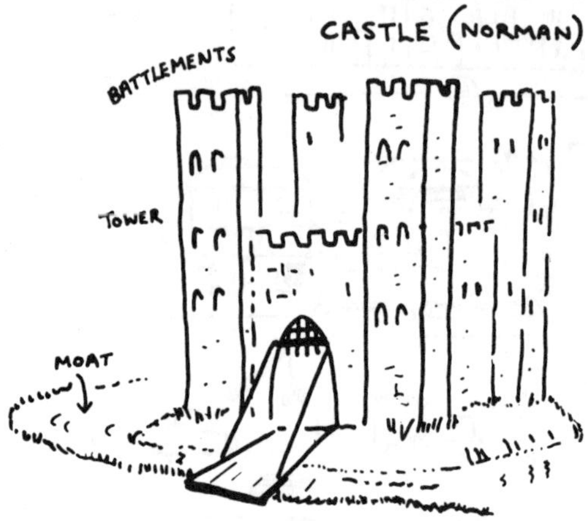

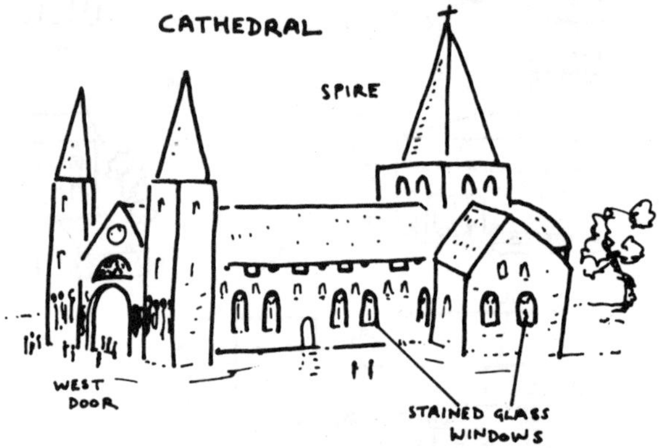

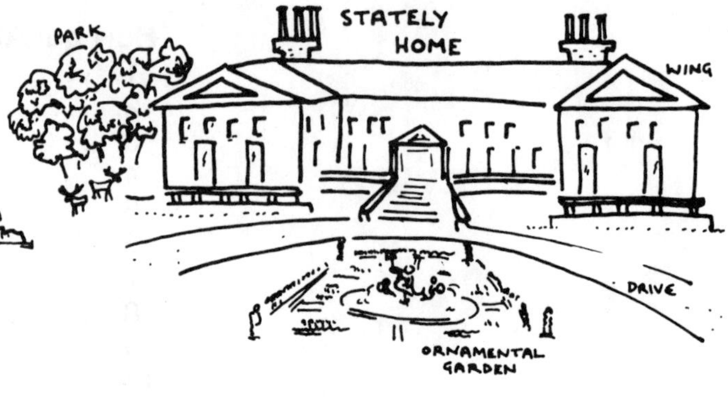

What are the most interesting buildings in your country?

Do you know anywhere like this? Which do you prefer? Are there good and bad things about each type of place?

1. picturesque
   half-timbered* cottages
   thatched roofs
   diamond-paned* windows
   low ceilings with oak beams

2. narrow lanes
   small harbour
   little quay
   stone cottages
   cobbled streets

3. red brick factories
   tall chimneys
   terraced houses
   warehouses

4. new shopping centre
   big bright shop windows
   estate of modern bungalows
   park with swings

ACTIVITY

1. **Write a short description of a building you like.**
2. **Write a short dialogue using the words:**
   bungalows   bulldozer   suburbs

22 Postcards and Letters

Complete the postcard from the word lists below:

Dear...........
I'm having........(1)......... time here in........(2)......I'm
staying at a ....(3)..........in..............(4).............The
weather is ....(5).....so/but I'm ....(6)........ a lot.
Yours,
....

1. a good	2. France	3. hotel	4. the mountains.
a terrific	Italy	camp site	the north.
an exciting	England	youth hostel	Florence.
an interesting	Greece	caravan site	a very beautiful area.
5. good	6. sunbathing		
hot	skiing		
snowy	sightseeing		
wet	walking		

You can expand this by using some of these phrases:
Thanks very much for your card.
It's good to hear from you again.
I was very glad to hear from you again.
I'm very glad that you ...
I'm sorry to hear about ...
You must come and visit us.
We may see you in ...
... sends his best wishes.
Best wishes to ...

Notice the position of the address on the letter:

12 Orchard Street
Maidstone
Kent

20 March 1980

Dear Jim,

and on the envelope:

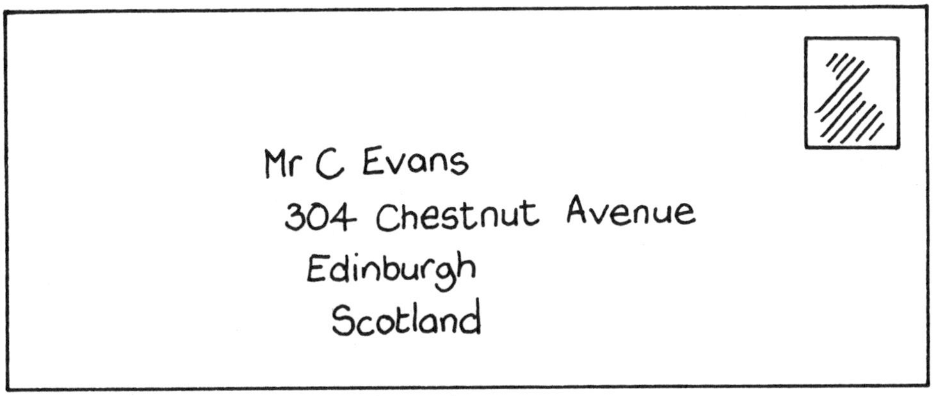

ACTIVITY

1. **Reply to this letter you have received from a friend:**

Dear

Sorry I haven't written for a long time. I've been busy because I've got a new sales job which is hard work but very interesting. We've also just got back from holiday in Scotland; it was very enjoyable – until I broke my leg!

Sarah sends her best wishes. I hope your parents are fit and well. I'm doing a lot of travelling in the new job so I may see you later in the year.

Yours,

2. **Write a short dialogue using the words:**
   best wishes   a long time   I'm glad

23 Hobbies

In pairs discuss your hobbies, using the language below:

What are your interests/hobbies?
What do you do in your spare time?

I like / I'm keen on / I'm interested in / I'm good at / I'm fond of / I enjoy

- playing the piano/guitar, singing.
- listening to classical/folk/pop/opera music
- photography: movie camera/colour slides/prints/developing and printing.
- sailing, fishing, gardening, food and wine, cooking, collecting silver/prints/glass/stamps/dolls.
- sports, playing tennis/football/bridge, athletics, swimming, skating.
- dancing, acting, amateur dramatics.
- drawing, painting, dressmaking, model making.
- keeping birds/dogs/horses/tropical fish.
- reading about/studying ancient history.
- going to the cinema/theatre.

Do you enter competitions?

I do it
- for fun/for enjoyment/for my own interest/for relaxation.
- to get away from it all/to take my mind off work.

Why do you like it so much?

- It's very relaxing, challenging. It's a complete change from work.
- It takes a lot of time/concentration/patience.

Who is your favourite sportsman/composer/painter/actress . . .?

My favourite . . .

What do you need for football? / fishing?

Kit: boots, shorts etc.
Gear: tackle, rod, line etc.

How do you make pottery?

You need . . . First you . . . and then you . . .

WORD CHECK

What hobbies do you connect with these pictures?

ACTIVITY

1. **Think of words and phrases to help you describe *your* hobby to the class.**
2. **Write a short dialogue using the words:**
   studying patience relaxation

24 Parties

Invitations

John? This is Patty. We're having a little party on Friday to celebrate the end of the week. Can you come?

Thanks. I'd love to. What time shall I come round?
or
I'd love to but I'm afraid I've arranged . . ./ got to . . .

Good. See you nine-ish/about nine.
or
Oh, what a pity. Never mind. Next time perhaps.

Flat 5
Sandgate House
Hill Road
Folkestone

You are invited to SHEILA'S FLAT WARMING PARTY on Saturday, 5thJuly 1980
8 pm onwards
RSVP

Dear Sheila
Thanks very much for the invitation. I'd love to come. Look forward to seeing you on the 5th.
Yours,
Mary.

Invite a friend to your party.

What sort of party?

Where might you wear a dinner jacket or long dress and jewellery?
a clown costume with a big red nose?
jeans and a warm sweater?

What sort of clothes would you wear to a wedding reception?
an office party?

Do you usually take presents to a birthday party?
a dinner party?
a flat warming*?
a 'Saturday night' party?

Food and drink

What do you usually serve at a party?

snacks, buffet supper, 'help yourself', cheese dips, sausages on sticks;
big cans of beer, a 'bottle' party*, home-made punch (be very careful – you don't know what's in it!)

Conversation

I'm sorry I'm late. { I got held up at the office. / The traffic was terrible. / The babysitter couldn't find us. } — Never mind. Have a drink.

Would you like to dance? — { Certainly. / No thanks. / Not at the moment, thanks. / I don't dance. / It's a bit hot. / I'm having a little rest. }

Goodnight, and thank you very much. We have had a lovely time.

TO TALK ABOUT

What happens at children's parties in your country?

Did you have a party on your 18th birthday?
the night before you got married?
when you moved into a new house?
last Christmas?

What happened?

ACTIVITY

1. **Write an invitation to someone in your class. Give it to them and wait for a written reply.**
2. **Write a note inviting a business visitor to dinner at your home. (Don't forget time/place/any other details.)**
3. **An English friend has written and invited you to a party in a fortnight. You can't go. (You must give a good reason.)**
4. **Write a short dialogue using the words:**
   invitation about 8 p.m. look forward to

25 Theatre and Shows

Theatre

Practise this dialogue in pairs.

I'm going to the theatre tonight.
What are you going to see?
Seagulls on Flowergate Roof.
Who's it by?
It's by a young playwright called Peter O'Milne.
Who's in it?
It's starring Patrick Hargreaves.
What sort of play is it?
It's a comedy.
It's had very good reviews.

People

Behind the scenes: the producer, stage manager and stage hands, set designer and costume designer, make-up artists, lighting team, prompter.

Out front: the man/woman in the box office*, programme sellers, usherettes.

On stage: actor, actress, hero, villain, the star of the show.

Booking seats

Can I have two tickets in the circle for Saturday's matinée please?

Certainly. There's 5 and 6 in row K in the upper circle at £3 each, or 28 and 29 in the middle of row B in the front circle at £4 each.

stalls, front circle, upper circle, balcony, box, row.

Opinions

Well, what did you think of it?

I enjoyed it very much.

I liked { the music. / the sets. / the costumes. / the story. }

It was { very sad. / quite funny. / most spectacular. / a bit boring. }

Opera

conductor, orchestra, overture, aria, chorus, soloists, soprano, contralto, tenor, bass; cheering and applause, encore, curtain call.

Cinema

feature film*, short (film), movie, cartoon, in technicolor, screen, foyer, usherette, director, producer, script, dubbing, subtitles.

ACTIVITY

1. **Tell the class about a show you have seen and complete this dialogue:**

   Me: Have you been to the theatre/cinema recently?
   You:
   Me: Who is it by? What's it about?
   You:
   Me: Did you like it?
   You:

2. **Which of these factors influence your enjoyment of a night at the theatre/cinema most?**

   a) the place you sit
   b) the reputation of the actors
   c) the reviews you have read
   d) the person you go with
   e) whether you are familiar with the play/story

3. **Connect the name of the show with the description and with the review:**

Saturday Night Rave	A thriller	'I laughed till the tears ran down my face.'
Aida	A musical	'Spine-chilling* – the man next to me fainted!'
Murder at Midnight	A pantomime	'A delightful evening – I sang and danced all the way home.'
The Merry Widow	A comedy	'A show of tremendous vitality and energy. Rock at its best.'
Macbeth	An operetta	'Powerfully dramatic.'
No Sex Please We're British	A tragedy	'Ideal entertainment for all the family.'
Cinderella	An opera	'Magnificent sets and superb singing – a very moving performance.'

4. **Write a short dialogue using the words:**
   spectacular reviews applause

26 In the Restaurant

Restaurant au Connell

Will you order now sir?
Yes, I'd like . . . to start with, followed by . . . with . . .

Yes sir, and to drink?
A bottle of . . .

Certainly sir. How would you like your steak? Rare? Medium? Well done?
Rare please.

****

Finished sir?
Yes. That was very nice.

Would you like a dessert from the trolley?
No. Just cheese and biscuits please.

****

Coffee sir?
Yes. I'll have it black please.

Order your meal from the menu.

MENU
£6.00
Fruit Juice
Soup of the Day
Prawn Cocktail
Melon
* * * * * *
Fillet of Plaice
Roast Beef and Yorkshire Pudding
Lamb Chops with Mint Sauce
Rump Steak
* * * * * *
Choice of Vegetables
peas, carrots, beans, onions, broccoli, mixed Salad
Potatoes – boiled, roast, sauté, french fried
* * * * * *
Trifle
Fresh Fruit Salad
Gateau
* * * * * *
Cheese and Biscuits
Coffee

WINE LIST
Wide choice of beers, spirits and liqueurs available
* * * * * *
Beaujolais '78 5.20
St. Emilion '77 4.60
Liebfraumilch '76 4.80

Eating out

go out for a meal ... book a table for two ... order the first and second course ... order the dessert ... ask for the bill ... 'Is service/VAT* included?' ... leave a tip.

Choose a restaurant!

Pete's Place Self Service
Omelets, sausages, pies & chips with everything.

Pete's Plaice Fish'n' chips
Plaice/cod and chips freshly fried

Pete's Diner – All American
Giant Hamburgers with beans, followed by homemade Apple Pie

Ying Chow Pete Chinese Take Away
Best oriental cuisine, take away service, open all night

Pete's Bombay Curry House
Finest curries in Town. Fully licensed.

What's your favourite restaurant like?

romantic atmosphere ... interesting menu ... good range of wines ... candlelight and soft music ... good service ... very reasonable prices.

TO TALK ABOUT

Where do you usually go for a) a quick snack b) a special meal in your country?
Do you think that people go out to eat more or less frequently than a few years ago?

ACTIVITY

In threes:

1. **Use the menu to order a meal – someone must be the waiter.**
2. **Describe your favourite restaurant to a friend.**
3. **Write a short dialogue using the words:**
   medium rare   slow service   nice atmosphere

27 Keeping Fit

What's the matter?

Oh I'm so overweight. I get out of breath walking to the fridge.

You're out of condition. Give up smoking and try
- doing some exercises.
- running on the spot.
- touching your toes.
- bending and stretching.
- breathing deeply.
- jogging.
- physical training.

You should
- go on a diet.
- give up beer, chocolate, fatty foods.

ACTIVITY

1. Healthy eating

In pairs choose a day's menu for two people. You are both hungry people. One of you has a sweet tooth. The other one likes meat very much. You must have the same meals. Your menu should come to 900–1000 calories each.

	Calories		*Calories*		*Calories*
cornflakes	210	salad	10	peas	70
milk ($\frac{1}{4}$ litre)	150	soup	73	cheese	90
sugar (spoonful)	55	grilled chicken	152	cake	140
bread and butter	80	hamburger	225	apple	40
jam/marmalade	30	veal (cheese on top)	260	fruit juice	50
bacon and eggs	300	pork chop	400	whisky	180
boiled egg	80	herring	220	coffee (black)	5
ham sandwich	250	green vegetable	20	coffee (white)	40
steak and mushrooms	330	yoghurt	75	tea (milk, no sugar)	20
				beer	160

2. Yoga

The Head Stand

1. Kneel on the floor and bend forward with your forearms on the floor.
2. Rest the top of your head on the floor, inch forward with your feet and push your bottom into the air.
3. Gradually transfer your weight on to your forearms and take your feet off the ground.
4. Gradually straighten up until you are in a vertical position.

Explain (or demonstrate!) how to do:
The Bow

... lie ... reach back ... grasp feet ... raise trunk ... knees together ... slowly lower.

and *The Lotus*

.... legs straight ... ankle ... left thigh ... fold over right leg ... crosslegged ... hands ... relax.

3. **Write a short dialogue using the words:**
jogging diet non-fattening keep fit

28 Football and Tennis

Do you play either of these sports?

Football

team
goal keeper
full back
centre half
wingers
forwards
striker
defenders
reserve
football fans
supporters
referee

shorts
boots

score
miss
offside
handball
throw in
free kick
pass
header
shoot
tackle
foul
dive

'book' someone (yellow card)
send someone off (red card)

stadium
pitch
stands
goal
net
post
crossbar
penalty spot
corner flag
half-way line

United are leading 3–1
Arsenal won 2–0 (two-nil)
Liverpool beat Leeds 2–0
a 2–2 draw (2 all)

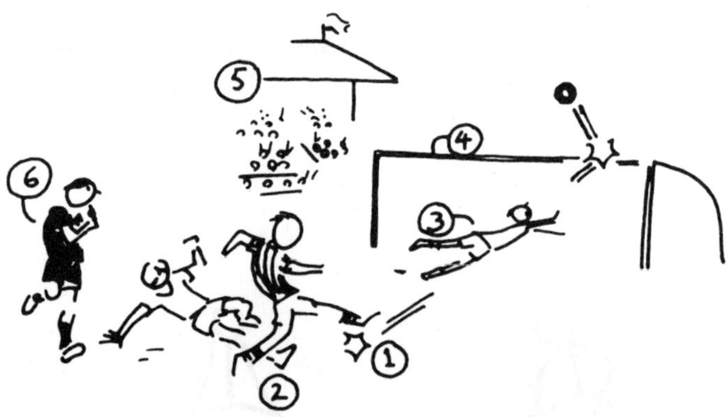

WORD CHECK

Find the words for these numbers:

1. ....
2. ....
3. ....
4. ....
5. ....
6. ....

A football commentary

. . . and from the free kick in mid-field, Lofty Chisholm dribbles upfield, beats Kirby . . . a hard tackle from 'Boots' Hartman . . . but Lofty passes to Milne . . . Milne out to Hargreaves on the wing . . . a high centre . . . Dickson goes up for it . . . a goal mouth scramble . . . Kirby gets a boot to it . . . the ball goes out to Milne again . . . oooh and a great shot towards the left hand post . . . Tyler dives . . . but it's in the net!! Milne has scored . . . a fantastic goal!! What a player!

Tennis

A tennis commentary

Lloyd serves to the left-hand court . . . a low forehand return from Wade . . . backhand cross court volley from Lloyd . . . splendid return down the line . . . Lloyd gets there . . . a lob to the back of the court . . . it's just out . . . love-fifteen.

singles
doubles
mixed doubles
racket and press
net
court
sideline
baseline
umpire
line judge

30–0 (thirty-love)
40–40 (deuce)
advantage to . . .
game
set
match

serve
backhand
topspin
forehand
smash
backspin
volley
lob
a long rally

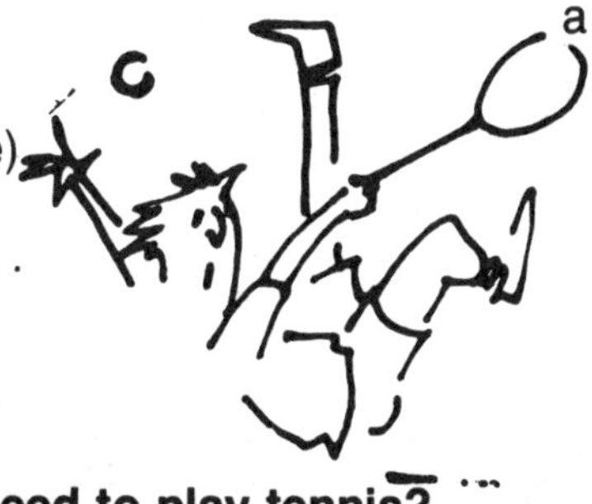

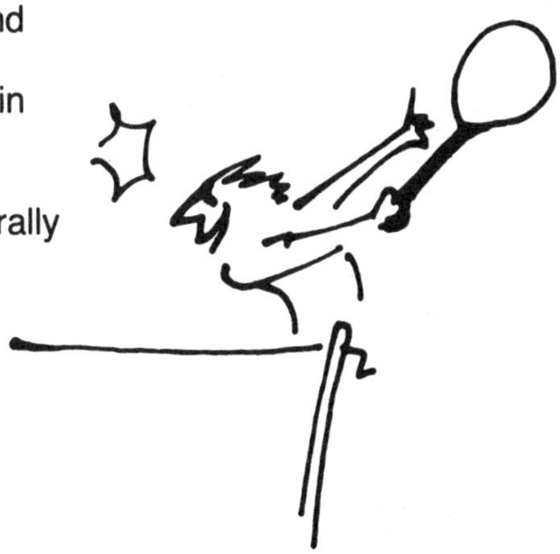

What do you need to play tennis?
Which do you enjoy most: singles?
doubles?
mixed doubles?

Have you ever been to a major football or tennis match? Who was playing? What was the result? Do you ever watch these sports on television?

TO TALK ABOUT

Is football hooliganism a serious problem? Can anything be done about it?
Top footballers and tennis players get paid far too much money. Do you agree?

ACTIVITY

Write a short dialogue using the words:
good shot net final score

29 Sports

WORD CHECK

Put the number to the name:

stick ___,
court ___,
running shoes ___,
winning post ___,
baton ___,
pads ___,
track suit ___,
bowling alley ___,
club ___,
diving board ___,
ring ___,
bat ___,
trunks ___,
net ___,
helmet ___,
pool ___,
pitch ___,
track ___,
glove ___,
wicket ___,

What sports not shown here are important in your country?
Can you name three new sports?

Athletics

Can you describe the following events?

Track events:
sprints/middle distance/long distance races
hurdles
relay
marathon

Field events:
putting the shot
throwing the discus
pole vault
long/high jump
throwing the javelin

ACTIVITY

1. Olympic Games

Work in groups.

You are the Policy Committee of the Olympic Council.
It is accepted that the Olympic Games are too big. Very great demands are made upon the resources of the host cities in terms of: a) money b) space.
Your task is to reduce the programme, to decide today which *five events* should be omitted from the programme. You should consider:

1. Physical factors (numbers of contestants, facilities needed).
2. The extent of the appeal of different events to all the people of the world.
3. National feelings and preference. Tradition.
4. The Olympic ideals of: a) individual excellence
   b) strict non-professionalism.
5. Finance, in particular television contracts.

OLYMPIC PROGRAMME

1. ARCHERY
2. ATHLETICS
3. BASKETBALL
4. BOXING
5. CANOEING
6. CYCLING
7. EQUESTRIAN (RIDING)
8. FOOTBALL
9. GYMNASTICS
10. JUDO
11. PENTATHLON
12. ROWING
13. SHOOTING
14. VOLLEYBALL
15. WATER POLO
16. WEIGHTLIFTING
17. YACHTING

Now report the recommendations of your group to the rest of the class.

2. **Write a short dialogue using the words:**

agility training facilities

30 Customs and Festivals

How many traditional holidays do you have each year?

Ways of celebrating

Processions:
carnivals, historical pageant, decorated floats.

Decorations:
flags, bunting, banners, masks, uniforms and costumes.

Lots of noise:
bands, dancing in the street, special songs, fireworks, everyone goes wild.

It's an old tradition . . . it goes back to the Middle Ages . . . it dates from the 19th century. An old superstition . . . an old religious custom.

Do you have these traditions? Sometimes it's difficult to remember their religious significance.

This is a very ancient tradition.
Do you have a Spring festival?
What do you do on May 1st?

This was a political event – an attempt to blow up the King and Houses of Parliament in 1605 – now celebrated by children in a bonfire and fireworks party.

What old traditions do you have at Christmas?

It is a Scottish custom to visit with coal and salt.
Do you have any New Year customs?

ACTIVITY

1. **List the special customs and festivals which *you* celebrate? Think of words and phrases to help you describe a special custom to the rest of the class.**
2. **Discuss how these festivals have changed in the last twenty years.**
3. **Write a short dialogue using the words:**
   custom superstition celebrate

31 Newspapers

People

Who works for the paper?
editor, sub-editor, editorial staff, reporters, journalists, columnists, owner.

Papers

Fleet Street (where the editorial offices are);
The Times, The Daily Telegraph, The Guardian (serious press);
Daily Mail, Daily Mirror, The Sun, Daily Express (popular press);
The Observer, The Sunday Times, Sunday Telegraph, News of the World (Sunday papers).

Content

editorials, features, articles (political, foreign/domestic news, economic, etc), sports/fashion pages, advertisements, notices of births, marriages and deaths, obituaries, pin-ups, arts reviews, letters to the editor, job advertisements (Situations Vacant), personal/gossip column, women's page, cartoons, TV and radio programmes, weather report/forecast, crossword, colour/special supplement.

page, headline, column, paragraph, line, photograph.

Reputation and approach

right/left wing, middle of the road, unbiased, independent, government run, satirical, sensational, gives good coverage of . . . , takes a strong line on . . .

Magazines

'glossy' magazines: features, quizzes and competitions, stories about the stars, romantic stories, lots of colour photographs, horoscopes, recipes, strip cartoons.
trade/specialized magazines.

TO TALK ABOUT

What are the most important papers in your country?
Are they politically biased?
What makes a good newspaper?

ACTIVITY

1. **Where in the paper would you expect to find the rest of these stories, and can you say anything about the types of newspaper?**

a) . . . was sent off after kicking the goalkeeper in the . . .

b) . . . 's tragic death at such an early age is a loss to the whole music world.

c) 1 down. Useful method of air transport (10)

d) Gold buttons and bright contrasting colours are in for men's trousers this spring.

e) A well written, powerful adventure story based on the author's own experiences in Russia during . . .

f) . . . speech which put most of the House to sleep he proposed another typically unrealistic and short-sighted piece of socialist propaganda.

g) PRIME MINISTER ANNOUNCES RESIGNATION

2. **Where in a magazine would you find the following lines?**

a) Coat, lady's dark brown suede, as new, length 42 in. £65 o.n.o. (or nearest offer)

b) Sincere gentleman wishes to meet lady, early 40s, with sense of humour, intelligence and real interest in the arts.

c) Put any left-overs you have into a large pot and add . . .

d) Applicants should have at least 5 years relevant experience.

e) The fiery planet, Mars, continues to dominate your home life and it is essential you . . .

3. **Where are these newspapers published?**

Al-Ahram
Le Figaro
The People's Daily
Herald Tribune
La Stampa
Pravda

4. **Read these headlines:**

POPSTARS SPLIT UP 'All Over Now' laments Decca's Darling
DRIVING TEST CRASH CASE – INSTRUCTOR CLEARED

a) Work together to produce the possible background to these headlines.
b) Write a 150-word article to fit one of the headlines.

5. **Write a short dialogue using the words:**
freedom of the press satirical headlines

32 Television and Radio

Programmes

soap opera*, family shows, plays, films, features, sports programmes, news, weather forecast, party political broadcasts, adverts, comedy, children's programmes, educational programmes, westerns, detective programmes, horror films, cartoons, panel games, documentaries, variety shows.

People

Put the right person against each programme:

news reader, presenter, compere, chairman, questionmaster, disc jockey, interviewer, commentator.

1. variety show ....
2. quiz ....
3. pop music ....
4. interview with celebrity ....
5. discussion ....
6. documentary ....
7. sports report ....
8. news ....

Describing a programme

. . . starring . . . also in the cast . . . with guest celebrity . . . produced by . . . research by . . .

popular, long running*, twice weekly, live/recorded, has catchy theme music;
a *serial* is a programme with a developing story: a *series* is a number of separate programmes with the same theme.

TO TALK ABOUT

1. **What sort of programmes would you expect to see** several times a day?
   just before a general election?
   on Saturday afternoons?
   in the middle of other programmes?
   very late at night?

2. **Are these things true about TV in your country?** . . . high standard . . . too much American influence . . . radio gives better variety . . . very educational . . . good balance of serious and light programmes . . . too much sex and violence . . . good family entertainment.

ACTIVITY

1. **In pairs, match the titles to the programme notes.**

   Programme notes

   1. This week's programme goes off the beaten track* in rural France and visits a brand new resort on the Red Sea coast.
   2. Captain Coburn has plenty of trouble on his hands when Chief Cochise goes on the warpath.
   3. Elliott M. Estes made it all the way from the factory floor to the top of the second business empire in the world.
   4. 1886: Marya Sklodowska is a governess on a country estate outside Warsaw. Her hope is to save enough money to study science, but as a woman, her only chance to do this is to follow her sister to France.
   5. News from London and studio and film features from all corners of the country.
   6. Leading art historians talk about the superb anatomical drawings of Leonardo da Vinci.
   7. In this tense drama two planes, a Navy jet and a transcontinental airliner, head towards a meeting in the air lanes.
   8. A tiny red dot in the sky has for centuries filled people's imaginations with little green men and strange canals.

   Titles

   A. 21.50 *Marie Curie.* A repeat showing of the widely acclaimed series in five parts first shown last summer.
   B. 17.05 *Horizon: The Planet Mars.*
   C. 20.00 *Americans.* A new series.
   D. 22.40 *Arena: Art and Design.*
   E. 18.50 *Saturday night at the movies: The Crowded Sky.*
   F. 17.55 *Nationwide.*
   G. 15.00 *Weekly cinema: Forty Guns to Apache Pass.*
   H. 18.10 *Holiday* introduced by Cliff Fairmore.

2. **Work in small groups and make a list of the ways in which television can influence people's lives.**

3. **Write a short dialogue using the words:**

   long running series starring

33 Telephone

Getting a number

To look up a number, find the person's name in the area telephone directory.
Each town has a code.
To ring a number in Birmingham (e.g. 246 8091) look up the Birmingham code in the small Dialling Codes book. Dial the code and then the number.
To find a taxi/doctor/hotel etc, look in the Yellow Pages in the big telephone directory.

On the phone

The other person may not know you, he/she cannot see you, the line may not be very good, so think what you want to say in advance (especially any questions you want to ask). Speak *clearly.* Speak *slowly.*

Public telephones in England are usually in red phone boxes. The things which you can hear (signals) differ from country to country, but there is always:

1. a *dialling tone*, which means you can dial a number.
2. a *ringing tone*, when the connection has been made but before anyone answers.
3. an *engaged signal* (sometimes called a *busy signal*) indicating that the other person's telephone is being used.
4. A *number unobtainable signal.* This can mean for example that the other person's telephone is out of order.

When you ring someone:

If you are friends with the person at the other end: This is Jim./Jim here./Jim Brown here.

If it's a business call and they don't know you: My name is Brown./This is Mr Brown of Portly Puddings.

and then:

Is that the International Hotel?
May I speak to Mr Davidson please?
I'm ringing about . . .
Can I have the reception desk?
I'd like to speak to someone in your Sales Department please.
Could you take a message, please? Tell him Mr Brown rang about . . .
Will you ask him to ring me back please?
This is a very bad line. Could you speak up please?
I'll ring off now and call you again tomorrow.

When the phone rings, pick it up and say:

Jim here
or: Jim Brown
or: 55061 (double five o six one)
or: Brown speaking
or: Export Sales Department. Can I help you?

The operator, secretary or receptionist may say:

I'm sorry, the line's engaged.
Hold the line please (i.e. please wait a moment).
Can I take a message?
Could you call again after 3 o'clock?
I'm putting you through.
I'm trying to connect you.
You're through now.
I'm sorry, you've got the wrong number.

ACTIVITY

1. **Make a business appointment by telephone with Mr Jackson of Powerhouse Tools. You have never met him before.**
2. **Phone your friend Anita and arrange to meet at the weekend.**
3. **Ring the Speediclean Dry Cleaners to ask if your suit is ready.**
4. **Phone your teacher to explain why you aren't at school.**
5. **Call your girl/boy friend. She/he is in the bath. Her/his mother answers the phone.**
6. **Write a short dialogue using the words:**
   code wrong number ring back

34 Education

School

In Britain: school compulsory from 5 to 16, playgroup, kindergarten, junior school, comprehensive school/secondary school/grammar school (State system), public school (which is private!).

What is the school system in your country?

lessons, homework, games, teachers, school uniform (did you wear one?).

Discipline and punishment

extra work, detention, corporal punishment (the cane).

Subjects

Which subjects did you study?
languages, maths, sciences;
compulsory subjects (everybody had to do them);
optional subjects (you could choose between them).

What was your favourite subject?
What did you hate?
chemistry (labs), woodwork, metal work, art, geography, history, music, cooking, religious instruction, PT (physical training), sex education, social studies.

Higher education

I studied electrical engineering at Liverpool for three years.
university, college of education, technical college, polytechnic*, Open University*, evening classes, day release*.

apply for a place to read/study . . . (mathematics), go for an interview, do a course in literature/car maintenance, go to lectures and tutorials, take an exam, pass/fail an exam, take one's finals, get a first/second/third class degree*, a BA in English, a BSc in Chemistry, a diploma in . . ., do research, postgraduate study, higher degree (MA, MSc, PhD).

TO TALK ABOUT

10.5% of school leavers in the UK go on to university. 14.3% are involved in full-time education at the age of 20.

% of children aged under 4 who go to school	**1951:** 6.9	**1977:** 24.9
number of UK students in higher education	**1951:** 130,000	**1977:** 524,900
number of pupils per teacher (primary)	**1951:** 30	**1977:** 24
(secondary)	**1951:** 21	**1977:** 17
% in comprehensive (State secondary schools)	**1951:** 37.7	**1977:** 79.9

Are these trends the same in your country?

ACTIVITY

1. **Work in a small group and decide what a good education is. What are the most important things a young person should learn at school?**
   1. ....
   2. ....
   3. ....
   4. ....
2. **What are the five most important qualities of a teacher?**
3. **Write a short dialogue using the words:**
   secondary school teachers subject

35 Jobs

Possible company structure

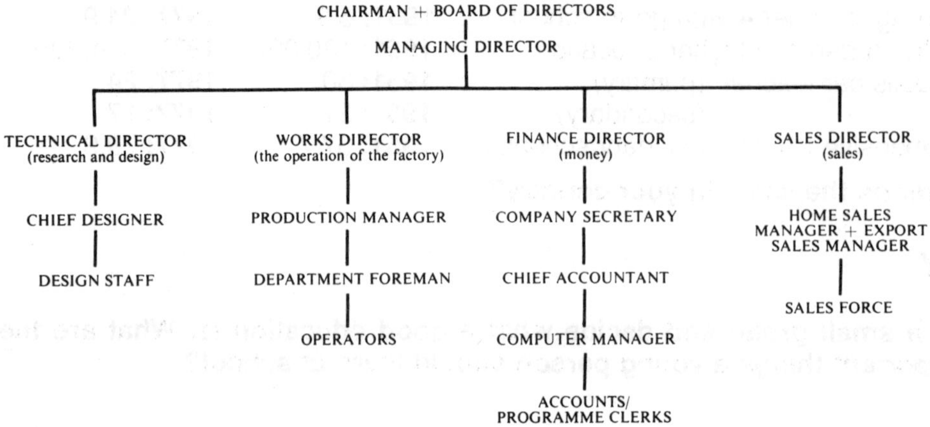

What do you do?	I'm a { salesman. / secretary. } I'm an engineer. I work for A.B.C.
Where do you work?	I work in a { factory / shop } in London. I work in an office. I'm a production manager with X.Y.Z. in London. I'm in the mining division.
What does your job involve?	My job involves { travelling around Europe. / helping sick people. / making decisions about . . . / studying reports. } I'm responsible to (someone) for (something). I'm responsible to the Marketing Manager for sales in my area.
Who/What do you deal with?	I deal with { overseas clients. / angry customers. / the technical side. / people who want . . . }
What is the job like?	The job is { very rewarding (job satisfaction/money). / interesting/challenging. / boring/routine. / very time-consuming. / I'm always under pressure. }
How big is your office?	My department consists of { 3 secretaries. / 50 clerks. / 4 salesmen. }

Fringe benefits/Perks (things in addition to your salary)

company car, expense account, recreation facilities, etc.

The fringe benefits are good/reasonable/miserly/non-existent!
I get ten weeks holiday a year . . .there's a pension scheme . . .we can buy our products cheaply.

Describing a firm/company

white collar workers*, manual workers, salary, wage, commission, bonus scheme, worker participation.
work on site, outdoor/indoor work, office work, a desk job.

Our company { specializes in . . . / produces parts for . . . / sells and services . . . machines.

There is a lot of competition/We have a monopoly/We are one of the biggest . . ./It's a small company.
We are a subsidiary of a Japanese firm.
We have subsidiaries in Denmark and Norway.

The end . . . .

retire at 65, 'golden handshake', made redundant, resign, get the sack.

ACTIVITY

1. **Which is the 'odd job out' in each line?**
   e.g. baker, greengrocer, *accountant,* carpenter.
   a) psychiatrist, vet, auditor, surgeon.
   b) draftsman, chemist, surveyor, architect.
   c) welder, waiter, chef, farmer.
   d) policeman, banker, traffic warden, referee.
   e) stockbroker, cashier, lawyer, economist.
   f) pilot, stripper, broadcaster, clown.
2. **Interview your neighbour about the sort of job he/she has or would like to have.**
3. **In writing, describe your job, where you work, your responsibilities, problems and rewards.**
4. **Write a short dialogue using the words:**
   responsible to time-consuming rewarding

36 Interviews and Job Prospects

One side of the interview: the interviewers

Good morning, Mr . . . Please take a seat.
My name is Robson and this is my colleague Mrs Knott.
Why are you interested in this job?

Are you prepared {
- to travel/to work overseas?
- to go on courses?
- to serve an apprenticeship?
- to do a probationary year?

This is a go-ahead company . . . we are expanding/opening new branches/taking over other companies.

What is your {
- present position/job/company?
- experience?

Do you like responsibility?
Why do you want to leave your present job/company?
Tell us something about yourself.
Are you ambitious? What do you hope to become?
Have you got any questions you'd like to ask us?
If we offered you the job, when would you be free to join us?
Thank you for coming. We'll let you know as soon as possible.

The other side: the applicant

I've been {
- a . . . for 3 years.
- responsible for . . .

I took my (qualification) in 1972.
Your company has a very good reputation.
The prospects in my present job are not very good.

What are the {
- prospects
- fringe benefits*
- holidays

} like?

Can you tell me more about {
- the job?
- the company?
- the prospects?

I'm interested in . . .

I want to {
- get on.
- earn more.
- get more job satisfaction.

I want more responsibility.

I hope to become {
- Managing Director.
- Head of Research.
- Chairman.

see an advertisement . . . fill in an application form . . . invited to an interview . . . put on the short list . . . final interview.
'We are very pleased to be able to offer you the job.'
'We're very sorry there has been a lot of competition and I'm afraid we can't offer you the job.'
salary negotiable between £10,000 and £12,000 p.a. . . . three months' notice* . . . good prospects for promotion . . . annual increment . . . 10% commission . . . wait for 'dead men's shoes'*.

Qualities of the candidate

extrovert/outgoing, very quiet, intelligent/bright
quick to learn, a bit slow, has got a lot of initiative, very thorough, a 'whizz kid'*.

ACTIVITY

1. **Fill in an application form giving curriculum vitae and references.**

APPLICATION FORM (Write in capitals)
Position applied for ....
Surname .... Other names..........
Age .... Sex .... Marital status..........
Education ....
Professional Qualification ....
Previous Experience ....
Languages ....
Present position and salary ....
Interests ....

2. A Job to apply for
Candidates work out a curriculum vitae and reasons for wanting the job.
Interviewing board prepare more background information and questions to ask the applicants.

American College Director
seeks
SECRETARY/P.A.
Friendly and attractive young person with excellent office skills needed from now until June, resuming in August for 1 year. Lively, friendly office in Gloucester Road. Frequent dealings with lecturers and students. Experience and/or training at university level useful.
SALARY £5,000
Call Mr. E. Vincent, 01-246 8035 at your earliest convenience.

3. **Write a short dialogue using the words:**
ambitious training scheme prospects

37 Meetings and Conferences

Are you going to the conference in April?

Yes. { I'm speaking on alternative energy. / I'm making a speech on energy. / I'm one of the delegates. }

What's the date of the next meeting?
What's on the agenda? (the order of topics for discussion)
Have you read the minutes of the last meeting?

put forward a point of view ... discuss it ... debate it ... argue about it ... support or oppose it;
propose a motion ... second* it ... vote on it ... a majority decision, a unanimous decision, the Chairman has the casting vote in case of a tie, vote for or against ... or abstain*.

People

Chairman, Vice-Chairman, guest speakers
The Secretary keeps the minutes (a record of the discussion).

Policy meeting to be held
March 7th
AGENDA
1. Apologies for absence
2. Minutes of last meeting
3. Matters arising –
   – report on the internal circuit
4. Publicity
5. A.O.B.
6. Date of next meeting

A meeting

The chairman may say:
Ladies and Gentlemen, I declare the meeting open.
Apologies for absence from Mr ...
I'd like to welcome Mr ... who is going to talk to us about ...
I now call on Mr ... to address the meeting.
The first item on the agenda is ...
I'd like to thank Mr ... on behalf of all of us for a very interesting talk.
Has anyone got any questions? Are there any questions?
Has anyone got anything to add? Mr ..., you have the floor.
Order! One at a time, please! Out of order! Keep to the point please.

We're short of time. I must ask you to be brief. Is there any other business?
We'll take a vote. Those in favour? Those against? Abstentions?

I declare the motion { carried unanimously. (Everyone agrees.)
carried } by 6 votes to 4.
defeated }

I now adjourn the meeting till (next Wednesday)/I declare the meeting closed.

The people at the meeting may say:
Mr Chairman! Can I come in here? Can I make a point?
I'd like to ask Mr ... if ...
Hear, Hear! I agree entirely.
I propose that we ... I second that.
What are your views on ...? In my opinion ...That's irrelevant. It's quite clear that ...
Can we get back to the point? The point is that ...
That's a very short-sighted view ... Can we reach a compromise?

WORD CHECK

Complete:
1) If everyone agrees, the decision is ...
2) I didn't want to vote Yes or No, so I ...
3) The ... are the record of the meeting.
4) Let's meet again after lunch. I ... the meeting till 2.30 p.m.

TO TALK ABOUT

What are the most difficult things about meetings or conferences with people from other countries?

ACTIVITY

1. **Elect a Chairman.**
2. **Propose the following motions and vote on them:**
   finishing school at 4 p.m. today
   opening/shutting the window
   adjourning for coffee.
3. **Produce an agenda for a meeting next Monday to discuss points of common interest.**
4. **Write a short dialogue using the words:**
   unanimous discuss it agenda

38 Sales, Production and Distribution

How does the finished product reach the shop? Describe this process.

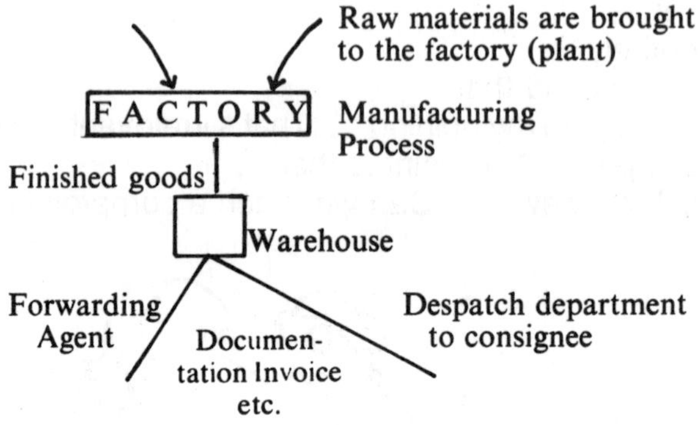

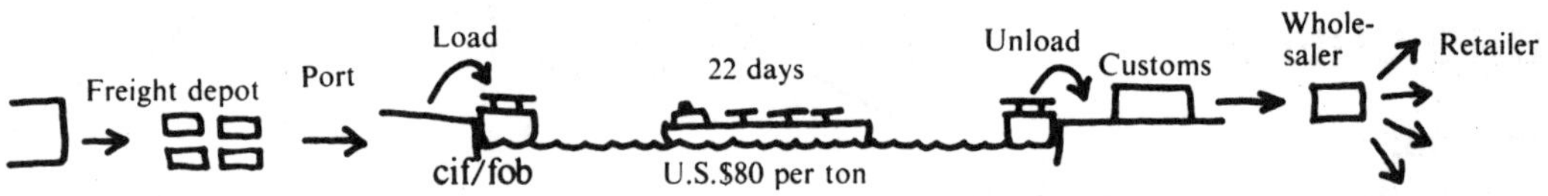

How is a product developed?
market research, field survey, R & D (Research and Development), innovation, technical achievement, major breakthrough.

How do sales and marketing teams try to get orders?
samples, promotion/publicity, advertising campaign, catalogue, brochure, 'door-to-door' sales, put in a tender (for a major project), competitive prices, undercut prices, discounts for bulk orders, hardware (equipment), software (know-how and servicing), guarantees, 'slush fund' (bribery and corruption), delivery times.

Ordering
make an enquiry, ask for an estimate/quotation, place a firm order, sign a contract.

Workers
work force, men on the shop floor*, trade unions, shop stewards, management, productivity agreements, piece work/time work.

Equipment
heavy machinery, tools, crane, forklift truck, pallet, container, container gantry.

Transport and distribution and payment

by road/rail/air/sea, finished goods are wrapped/packed, boxes, cartons, crates, airfreighted, containers are stuffed, container yard, freight rates, c.i.f./f.o.b. (cost, insurance, freight/free on board), Bill of Lading*/Airway Bill, loaded/unloaded, trans-shipped, cleared through customs, transit time, distributed to wholesalers/retailers, terms of payment, Letter of Credit* (30 days/90 days).

ACTIVITY

1. **Your company has just developed a pocket-sized article of general use and costing less than £1.**

   Work in groups.

   a) Decide: what your article is.
   how you are going to market it.

   b) You have received an enquiry from America (possibly 50,000 items). What information will you provide to try to win the order?

   c) Present your sales campaign to the other groups and persuade them to place orders.

2. **Write a short dialogue using the words:**
   raw materials wholesaler finished goods

39 Bank and Money

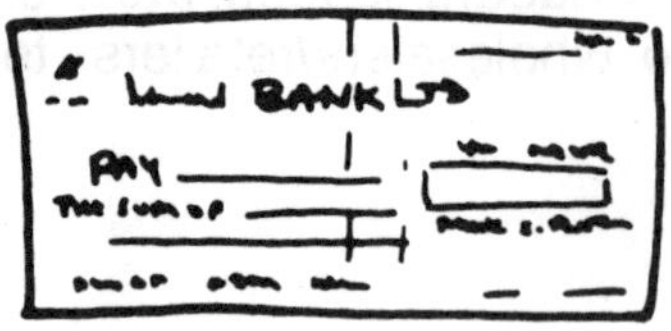

A cheque

Banknotes

7p (seven p). £4.70 (four pounds seventy or four pounds seventy p).
How do you say: 5p, 17p, £1.16, £25.03, £187.35½, US $60.25, 5.25 DM?

Bank

Bank Manager, cashier, cheque book, the Sandgate Road branch of Lloyds, current account/deposit account, pay in/withdraw, 'Can I have a statement please?', bank charges, 'in the red' (overdrawn), bank card, bank loan, bank rate, 8½% interest, interest rates are going up/down, investment advice, stocks and shares, Stock Exchange.

Do you have a bank account?

Buying and selling

pay by cheque, pay cash, hire purchase, put down/lose a deposit, instalment, bargains, sales, auction ('Going, going, gone!'), bulk purchase, discount.

Money and you!

cost of living, inflation, rising prices, devaluation/revaluation, retail price index, gross/net pay (take home pay), income tax, VAT (value added tax).

The company

shareholders, AGM (Annual General Meeting), profit and loss statement, balance sheet.

Foreign exchange

bank rate: £1 = DM 4.1 (4.1 marks to the pound).

Can I cash {a cheque / these travellers' cheques please?

Can you change 100 francs into pounds please?

Can I have 100 francs worth of pounds please?

What's the exchange rate today?

ACTIVITY

1. **Work in small groups.**
   You have £200 to spend on your 12-day European holiday:
   Switzerland 2 days; Germany 3 days;
   Yugoslavia 3 days; Greece 4 days.

   ### Exchange rate

Belgium	61.50 francs
France	9.26 francs
Germany	3.92 marks
Greece	69.00 drachma
Italy	1,635 lire
Japan	465 yen
Spain	155.50 pesetas
Switzerland	3.52 francs
United States	1.925 dollars
Yugoslavia	36.50 dinars

   Decide how much of each currency you require and ask the cashier to change £££s into money for the holiday.

2. **How might you buy** a) an antique Chinese vase?
   b) a car?
   c) 500 roubles?
   d) a pot of jam?
   e) a new suit?

3. A new pipe costs 400 plings now. I bought two of them last year when the price was 10% less. At that time I also bought a nice box of cigars and left the shop with only 20 plings change from a 500 pling note. As I was going to America the next day I changed this for $5. I want to buy another 5 pipes in the sales this year (there is a special 5% discount offer) and send them to my aunt in Madrid (the postage is 40 plings each). **Can you tell me how many dollars I need?**

4. **Write a short dialogue using the words:**
   account cash statement

40 Standard of Living

Levels of affluence

the standard of living is rising/falling . . . at subsistence level . . . can just make ends meet . . . reasonably well off/comfortably off/wealthy.

The big enemy: inflation

inflation is running at 9%, galloping inflation, prices and wages spiral.

What happens:
you get less for your money . . . your take-home pay is less in real terms . . . you are worse off.

So you:
go without . . ., cut down on . . ., you have to 'shop around'*, you can't afford to . . ., some people 'moonlight' (take a second job).

The situation sometimes leads to lack of investment/stagnation/depression/redundancy/unemployment.

Rumours of shortages lead to panic buying/stockpiling.

To counteract inflation or raise their standard of living people may get a rise/work overtime/get a cost of living rise. Salaries/pensions are linked to the cost of living index. The Government introduces price and wage freezes and incomes policies. Firms give their employees bigger perks, fringe benefits (allowances for entertainment, clothing, etc).
Heavy direct taxation leads to tax fiddles (non-declaration or false declaration of taxes) and the very rich look for tax havens* for their money.

Comparison of working time to buy various items

(Time in minutes)

	Milk	Beer	Petrol	Beef	Bread
Germany	5	18	5	143	15
France	7	13*	8	166	18†
Italy	9†	21	11†	184†	18†
United Kingdom	6	24†	7	146	9*
Denmark	4*	14	4*	136*	13

* shortest † longest

Consumer price index
1970 = 100

	August 1979	August 1978/August 1979 % change
Germany	117.2	+ 4.9
France	117.4	+10.5
Italy	178.7	+14.4
United Kingdom	171.2	+15.8
Denmark	149.9	+12.3

Can you draw any conclusions about prices/changes in the standard of living from these tables?

What are the effects on a) an exporter
b) a holidaymaker
c) 'the housewife' **if their currency suddenly becomes weaker?**

ACTIVITY

1. **Write a short dialogue using the words:**
well off   inflation   cost of living

Glossary

Unit		
1	**guinea pig**	small, fat, short-eared animal with almost no tail
	poodle	kind of dog (usually small) with thick curly hair
3	**double glazing**	a window with two sheets of glass for better insulation
4	**teatowel**	a towel used for drying dishes
	Hoover	a vacuum cleaner for cleaning carpets and floors (Hoover is a brand name)
	linoleum	a floor covering material
5	**Guinness**	a thick black beer originally made in Ireland
	licensing hours	(opening times are slightly different from place to place)
6	**Sellotape**	sticky tape (Sellotape is really a brand name)
	child allowance	a regular sum of money paid by the State to people with children
7	**special offers**	goods at reduced prices
	sausage roll	a sausage inside pastry
	Stilton, Cheddar, Leicester	different types of English cheese
	squash	a fruit-flavoured drink
9	**'a bit thick'**	(slang) rather stupid
10	**doctor's surgery**	the place where the doctor has his office and sees patients; a surgeon is the doctor who performs operations in a hospital
	Elastoplast	a small bandage, sticky on one side, to protect cuts (Elastoplast is really a brand name)
11	**stew**	a dish of meat or fish with vegetables cooked slowly for a long time
	custard	a yellow sauce made with milk, sugar and custard powder, poured over desserts such as apple pie
	marmalade	a preserve made from oranges or other citrus fruit; (a similar kind of preserve made from other fruit is called **jam**)
	Yorkshire pudding	a savoury pudding made from egg, flour and the juices of roast meat, and cooked in a very hot oven
13	**package tour**	a holiday where the price includes transport, accommodation and some meals
14	**to get your sea legs**	to get used to the movement of a boat so that you don't feel sick and can walk about when the boat rolls
15	**youth hostel**	a place where young people can have cheap accommodation when travelling (they share some of the domestic duties)
16	**double yellow lines** (on the road)	these mean parking is forbidden
	traffic warden	person in uniform, who has responsibilities in connection with traffic regulations
	lollipop lady	a woman who carries a big, round, yellow sign (like a lollipop) which tells traffic to stop and let children cross the road
17	**'P' registration**	the letter at the end of a car's registration plate tells you the year of its manufacture; 'P' is 1975/76
	AA	Automobile Association; an organization which helps motorists who belong to it
	'L' plates	learner drivers must have these signs (a big red letter 'L') at the front and back of their car
	MOT	Ministry of Transport; all cars over 3 years old have to pass an annual test of brakes, steering, bodywork etc.
18	**room service**	the possibility of having food and drink brought to your room
19	**Petticoat Lane**	a well-known street market

Unit		
20	**turnips, parsnips, sugarbeet**	all vegetables which grow under the ground; the parsnip is long and white and the turnip round with a darker colour; sugarbeet is white
21	**redevelopment**	renovation of buildings or a depressed area (e.g. slums)
	timbered	with a framework of wood
	diamond-paned	with diamond-shaped pieces of glass in a framework of lead
24	**flat warming**	a party to celebrate moving into a new flat (similarly, house warming)
	a 'bottle' party	a party to which the guests bring drinks
	home-made punch	a mixture of wine, spirits, fruit juice etc. made by the person giving the party
25	**box office**	the place in a theatre where you buy tickets
	feature film	a full-length film in the cinema programme
	spine-chilling	very frightening
26	**VAT**	value added tax; a tax imposed on most goods (some exceptions are food, books, children's clothes)
32	**soap opera**	very long running serial about the social relationships in a particular community
	long running	shown over a long period of time
	off the beaten track	out of the ordinary
34	**polytechnic**	a large technical college offering a range of degree level courses
	Open University	university whose students live at home and get tuition by correspondence and special TV and radio programmes
	day release	a system by which employees can take regular days off work to study
	degree	a university qualification; BA (Bachelor of Arts) and BSc (Bachelor of Science) are first degrees, usually obtained after 3 or 4 years' study; MA (Master of Arts) and MSc (Master of Science) are postgraduate degrees gained after (usually 2 more years; DPhil/PhD (Doctor of Philosophy) is a post higher degree given after several years of original research. In England people with such degrees are not usually called 'Doctor' unless they are in the academic world (or, of course, unless they are medical doctors).
35	**white collar workers**	workers with non-manual jobs
36	**fringe benefits**	(see Unit 35)
	three months' notice	you must tell your employers that you intend to leave at least three months in advance
	'dead men's shoes'	you have to wait for those senior to you to get so old that they retire before you can get promotion
	a 'whizz kid'	(slang) someone bright and dynamic who gets to the top very quickly and very young
37	**second**	to formally support a motion so that a vote can be taken
	abstain	to vote neither for nor against
38	**shop floor**	the part of the factory where production takes place
	Bill of Lading	a document signed by an officer on the ship to show that the goods are on board (Airway Bill is the equivalent for air transport)
	Letter of Credit	(in foreign trade) a method whereby the seller can get money from the buyer's bank as soon as he presents a Bill of Lading
40	**'shop around'**	go from shop to shop, looking for the best price
	tax haven	a place (outside the country where their tax is due) where wealthy people live to avoid paying heavy taxes